NETWORK CHAMPION

Interview Preparation Guide for the best in class Network Engineers

First Edition

ISBN: 9781652774587

COPY RIGHTS

About the Author

Wajid Hassan technical expertise spawns several years in building new Products and Solutions for IT Services, Telecommunications and Network Infrastructure verticals. He has been a strong proponent of Network Automation.

In the past he has worked at Tier 1 Telecommunication companies including AT&T, T-Mobile, Amazon Web Services as a Solution Architect and at US Government (USDA) developing and deploying innovative mobility and networking solutions. He has command on Mobility, Software Defined Networking, Virtualization, OpenStack, Linux Containers and VMware technologies. Having sound knowledge on the evolution of Cloud and market directions, on a day to day basis he provides technical solutions with practical approach.

He has dual Cisco Certified Internetwork Expert (CCIE) in Service Provider and Data Centre with additional CCIE security and CCIE Routing and Switching Written work completed. He is an AWS Certified Solutions Architect as well as VMware Certified Professional.

He has also served as a visiting faculty member at Bellevue College and taught at Indiana State University and Wichita State University. His undergraduate work on communication satellites earned him the 2008 IEEE-P Gold Medal Award. He has published several research papers. His two patents are pending approval.

He has a Master of Science degree in Electrical Engineering with emphasis on Digital Communication and Networking from Wichita State University. He is currently a PhD fellow at Indiana State University with specialization in Digital Communication. His PhD Dissertation is in Software Defined Networking, Machine Learning, Network Automation and Analytics,

Highly motivated in research, he has developed experimental Networking, Virtualization and Cloud Computing lab, provides guidance and mentors researchers in Networking, Cloud and Virtualization domains. He is the author of several books. He has several technical research papers published to his credit.

Wajid is a great proponent of Research & Development and is considered to be an excellent mentor in nurturing the new talent and building a high performing team. He has hands on experience in Python Scripting and Cisco, Juniper, Ericsson and Nokia equipment.

Contacting the Author

I'd be very interested to hear your comments and get your feedback on this book. Feel free to let me know what you think about the book or what additional items you would like to see in the next version of this book by sending me an email at wajid@logicfinder.net.

Customer feedback is critical to the success of this book; If you think you have found a technical error in this book, please send an email to wajid@logicfinder.net

We have provided an extensive list of resources that were used to answer some of the questions in this book. If we are missing a reference to your page, please reach out to us and we will gladly include the references with full credits here.

Acknowledgements

I would like to acknowledge the support or my associates and friends and family who have helped in making this book successful.

I would like to thank my wife Aiman, son Humza, My parents Khalid and Shahnaz, my brother Samad and sister Amber in their continuous support and for their encouragement.

My special thanks to Saba Asif and Tariq Mehmood who edited and provided details into the manuscript.

I have much gratitude to countless number of my associates who have read and help the manuscript and guided in helping to develop a network engineering better book.

Preface

This book is for individuals preparing for the network engineering interviews and discusses hundreds of scenarios based questions with simplified explanations to crack the interviews for the following Potential Job roles

- Network Engineer
- Level 1 Support Engineer
- Software Engineers building Networking products
- Test Engineers
- Network Development Engineers
- Support Engineers

In addition to that this book is also helpful for interviewers building and managing a team of network engineers such as

- Hiring Managers
- IT Recruiters
- Software Development Managers for Cloud
- Delivery Managers for Telecommunication and Service Provider networks

Although the tone of this book has been set for individuals starting out in the network engineering field but senior network engineers will also find it helpful to brush up their skills

The network engineering questions, and their answers will demonstrate the knowledge to deploy, maintain, secure and operate a medium-sized network using latest networking technologies.

We expect that these network engineers can design, install, configure, and operate LAN, WAN, and dial access services for small to large networks using some of these protocols: IP, VLANs, RIP, Ethernet, Access Lists Switching, Spanning Tree Protocol (STP), TCP/IP Protocol,IPv6,Routing Information protocol (RIP),Enhanced Interior Gateway Routing Protocol (EIGRP), OSPF, BGP, MPLS, QOS, Security, Load Balancers and last not least Network Automation.

Content

Figures

Tables

1. Introduction

Network Engineering is a broad and deep field of study. It has many protocols, standards and configuration methods depending upon the networking hardware vendors used in the network hence it's not easy to have a complete command on all technologies all the time, refresher is necessary for professionals working in network engineering domain.

From Trainee to Senior Network Engineers can get puzzled when going in for the Networking/Systems /Infrastructure interview as there is extreme amount of materials to prepare. I have seen many books and resources to crack the software engineering interviews but I have not seen the similar books on the network engineering subject hence this book helps to bridge that gap.

Network engineering is the super glue that binds the several components of the Infrastructure that builds todays Cloud Computing environments such as AWS, Service Provider Networks such as Comcast , Telecommunication networks such as AT&T and other enterprise IP networks.

The focus of the book is to help prepare the individuals for Network Engineering Interviews on the main network engineering technologies which are considered bread and butter.

Some individuals with less experience get disturbed when asked questions such as *"Can you explain a scenario where you may have handled a complex situation"*. Therefore, in this book we have discussed some of these scenarios and explain in brief the situation in which the answers were handled.

The book has about 500 questions divided in several categories such as Switching, Spanning Tree Protocol (STP), TCP/IP Protocol,IPv6,Routing Information protocol (RIP),Enhanced Interior Gateway Routing Protocol (EIGRP), OSPF, BGP, MPLS, QOS, Security, Load Balancers and last not least Network Automation. We will discuss each of these now

Chapter 2 introduces many common Scenario Questions, preparing for such questions will boost confidence in the candidates on how to answer the scenario based questions. These are double edged questions and can vary in details and depth. We have provided only sample answers. We encourage candidates to formulate their own answers. These are some questions that any Manager or Recruiter should also ask the potential employee.

Chapter 3 reviews the concepts of Switching , a very large and important topic asked in many interviews.

Chapter 4 This chapter is critical as many interview questions are asked on TCP/IP. Any Network or Systems Engineer should have a very good grasp on this subject.

Chapter 5 IPv6 is today widely implemented and many networks are required to support it. The importance arises because by the year 2001 there was a shortage of IPv4 space, Today IPv4 Address scheme is almost finished, there are no more IPv4 addresses that can be allocated.

Chapter 6 presents RIP one of the first and easier to implement routing protocols for less complex networks.

Chapter 7 presents EIGRP which was once a proprietary cisco protocol and still widely used.

Chapter 8 gets the reader to think about the most scalable and a very important networking routing protocol OSPF and used in hundreds of IP networks. It challenges the Network Engineers to think of several design scenarios and the asks them to resolve those scenarios.

Chapter 9 examines BGP which is the routing protocol of the internet and is essential in bring the network of the world together.

Chapter 10 is important for Network Engineers working for Service Providers as it raises questions on MPLS which reduces the latency in the complex networks.

Chapter 11 discussed QOS which manages data traffic to reduce packet loss, latency and jitter on the network. It is import for Cloud, Voice and Telecommunication networks and controls and manages network resources by setting priorities for specific types of data on the network.

Chapter 12 discusses several of the important Security scenario questions which are highly essential for improving the health and increasing the availability of the networks.

Chapter 13 Load Balancing is critical for WAN, cloud computing and Telecom networks as it balances the network load. We present many potential questions that can be discussed in an interview.

Chapter 15 is a very important for todays and future network as it discusses the motivations for Network Automation, discusses several libraries and important scripting and programming languages.

2.   Scenario Questions

1. **Tell me about yourself.**

Mention past experiences and proven successes as they relate to the position. Focus on strengths and abilities that you can support with examples.

2. **Why do you want to work at FAANG** (Facebook, Amazon, Apple, Netflix and Google (FAANG))?

The interviewer is looking for similar things whether asking about company or position. The hiring manager wants to: Learn about the career goals of the candidates and how this position fits into their plan.

3. **Why do you want this job?**

The truth is that many job seekers don't always have the time to fully research every company to which they apply. Besides, it can be discouraging to invest time and effort into researching a company just to find out that you did not land an interview. However, once the interview is a sure thing, it's time to take that step. You need to show the interviewer you've actually looked into what their company does. Fold this into your response to show that you are not delivering a memorized answer but speaking naturally as part of a conversation.

4. **What is your biggest strength? And your biggest weakness?**

At some point during the interview process, you may be asked to describe your personal strengths and weaknesses. Many job candidates are unsure about how to approach this question.

Here are some examples of strengths: Good Communicator, team player, time management abilities, conflict resolution, and ability to perform under pressure. You can think of more that have helped you shine in your career.

Here are some examples of weaknesses: Self-critical, perfectionism, take on too much responsibility etc. You can think of more weakness keeping in mind that these should not be related to the skills for the job that you are applying for.

5. **When was a time when you made a mistake? (**Be sure to tell them why it was a mistake, what the consequences were, but most importantly how you fixed things, made it right, and/or improved to make sure it didn't repeat)

6. **Tell me about a time you tried something and failed. (**The important part of this question is your reasoning for trying something new and what you learned from the failure.)

7. **Think of a difficult boss, professor or another person. What made him or her difficult? How did you successfully interact with the person?**

Every inch of your being wants to exclaim loudly what a nutjob your horrible boss was, but you need to figure out a way to talk positively about your bad experience. Come off as too critical, and recruiters won't want to move forward with your application. Having a clear plan of how you'll answer this inevitable question can help you make the right impression in your interview.

- Be Honest (Within Reason)
- Avoid Giving Unnecessary Information
- Turn the Negative into a Positive
- Remember What You Enjoyed
- Say What You're Looking for Instead

8. Tell me about a time you demonstrated initiative.

While working in AT&T MSP lab, Vendor was unable to deliver the product and hence took an initiative to write a protocol for video detection based on three features

9. Describe a situation when you have motivated yourself to complete an assignment or task that you didn't want to.

Give examples of times when you motivated yourself to reach a higher level of performance. This can be in times of adversity, but it doesn't need to have that framing. You can simply give a way that you motivate yourself on a daily basis to get work accomplished and deliverables completed. Unless you truly do not have any work examples, avoid personal examples.

10. Tell me about a time when you had competing priorities. How did you successfully manage those?

Focus on a time when you had to get others involved in setting and approving the prioritization of your work tasks and/or projects. Ideally, this would include your manager, but could also include other team members as well as external managers who are requesting your time.

Example:

"My job has multiple conflicting priorities where it can be difficult to know what is most important and urgent. My boss and I worked out an important/urgent scale for rating tasks so that it is clear what takes the highest priority. If something is both important and urgent, it gets highest priority. Important but not urgent is next and urgent but not important is next, then not important and not urgent is last. My boss knows the rating system and even codes request as IU, INU, UNI and NINU when sending them to me. As a result, my overall productivity in the past year has gone up considerably as benchmarked against prior to using our prioritization rating system"

11. Tell me about a time you improved a process at work.

Example Answer: I designed a document for junior engineers to troubleshoot common network problems and reverse engineer a problem.

12. Tell me about how you worked effectively under pressure.

I have worked in large teams and worked as a lead volunteer with XYZ. I don't get nervous handling large tasks or issues.

13. How do you handle a challenge? Give an example.

- Recall a challenge that was significant, but one that you consider a success.
- Don't just say what you did—explain how you did it.
- Emphasize the outcome and what you learned from it.

14. Give an example of a goal you reached and tell me how you achieved it?

Discuss the Method You Used to Reach Goals. There are a lot of different methods out there for achieving a goal. Many people use a visualization method to help make their goals a reality. However- if you want to impress the employer- you will need an answer that is more than 'I set a goal and thought about it and it happened.' Think about the steps you took to achieve a goal. Also think about the schedule you kept making it a reality. Time management and scheduling can make it much easier to actually achieve the goals you set and are a great detail to include in your answer to show the hiring manager you will be able to achieve other goals in the future. It is important your reply shows you understand the work that goes into the goals you set and your appreciation of the different potential outcomes available.

15. Describe a decision you made that wasn't popular and how you handled
   a. **Implementing it.**

16. Are you a team player?
Example Answer: "I understand and appreciate the fact that a team environment is both productive and efficient. I have the ability to compromise, show respect to others and listen to the needs of my teammates. While I can be a leader when necessary, I can also play an equal role on the team when the situation merits."

17. What do you do if you disagree with someone at work?

If you work with other human beings, disagreement is inevitable. And how you handle conflict is always an opportunity to come up with a better solution. If I were in an interview situation and were asked this question, I would say something like this: First it depends on the importance of the issue. Assuming it's a truly important issue, my first response is to understand the other person's position. And I'm fine with agreeing to disagree with mutual respect for one another.

What I avoid at all costs is making a disagreement personal and about the other person's character. No one wins in this situation. It's ultimately unconstructive and demoralizing to the larger organization.

18. Share an example of how you were able to motivate employees or co-workers.

Take the time to practice answering behavioral questions- such as the one listed above. Example: When motivating others, I tailor my responses to their personal strengths and capabilities. For example, at my last job, we had a team member that was never fully invested in the project. In order to motivate him, I made a conscious effort to stop by his desk every morning. I complimented him on the things he had done on the project and pointed out the skills I noticed he had that were essential to what we were working on. Over a period of a week or two, he started voicing his opinion and giving us creative ideas during every staff meeting. He felt valued and like he had something to offer, and he was no longer afraid to show it because he knew others felt the same way.

19. Have you handled a difficult situation? How?

Questions like this lets you show off your personality and allow you to be a real human being (as opposed to the perfect, error-free interviewing machine you're aiming to be). Everyone has had to deal with a difficult situation at work, when you talk about yours in an interview; you show a vulnerable, human side of yourself. Just be sure that the story you tell has an ending in which you overcome the difficult situation and learn an important lesson about yourself (which you should of course let your interviewer know about).

20. Tell me about a time you went above and beyond for a customer.

Example Answer: Many of our customers do not understand social media fully, which is why they come to us. I recently launched a private YouTube channel with video tutorials and how-tos. I sent the login information to all of our clients so that they could access the information on-demand. This effort saves them a phone call and email and also ensures that the information they need is at their fingertips, no matter the time of day or night. The response has been incredibly positive.

3. Switching

A. Spanning Tree Protocol (STP)

1. How STP works and what is its purpose?

Spanning Tree Protocol (STP) is a Layer 2 protocol that runs on bridges and switches. STP uses the Spanning-Tree Algorithm (SPA) to create a topology database of the network. To prevent loops, SPA places some interfaces into forwarding state and some interfaces into blocking state. The main purpose of STP is to ensure that loops are not created when there are redundant paths in the network.

2. Describe different types (STP, MSTP, RSTP) Cisco – PVST+/ Rapid PVST+?

1) STP—Spanning Tree Protocol (STP) is the original standard that provided a loop-free topology in a network with redundant links. It assumes one spanning-tree instance for the entire bridged network, regardless of the number of VLANs. STP can take 30 to 50 seconds to respond to a topology change.
2) MSTP—Multiple Spanning Tree Protocol (MSTP) maps multiple VLANs into the same spanning-tree instance.
3) RSTP—Rapid Spanning Tree Protocol (RSTP) is an evolution of STP that provides faster convergence than STP. RSTP is typically able to respond to changes within 3 × Hello times (default: 3 times 2 seconds) or within a few milliseconds of a physical link failure.
4) PVST+-- PVST+ (Per-VLAN spanning tree) is a Cisco enhancement of STP that provides a separate 802.1D spanning-tree instance for each VLAN configured in the network.
5) Rapid PVST+-- Rapid PVST+ is a Cisco enhancement of RSTP that uses PVST+ and provides a separate instance of 802.1w for each VLAN.

3. Describe the process of Root election?

A Root Bridge is a reference point for all switches in a spanning-tree topology. Across all connected switches a process of election occurs and the Bridge with the Lowest Bridge ID is elected as the Root Bridge. Bridge ID is an 8-byte Value that consists of 2-Byte Bridge Priority and 6-Byte System ID which is the burned in MAC address of the Switch.

4. Different port stages and timing for convergence?

The ports on a switch with enabled Spanning Tree Protocol (STP) are in one of the following five port states.

1. Blocking
2. Listening
3. Learning
4. Forwarding
5. Disabled

A switch does not enter any of these port states immediately except the blocking state. When the Spanning Tree Protocol (STP) is enabled, every switch in the network starts in the blocking state and later changes to the listening and learning states.

Blocking State

The Switch Ports will go into a blocking state at the time of election process, when a switch receives a BPDU on a port that indicates a better path to the Root Switch (Root Bridge), and if a port is not a Root Port or a Designated Port.

A port in the blocking state does not participate in frame forwarding and also discards frames received from the attached network segment. During blocking state, the port is only listening to and processing BPDUs on its interfaces. After 20 seconds, the switch port changes from the blocking state to the listening state.

Listening State

After blocking state, a Root Port or a Designated Port will move to a listening state. All other ports will remain in a blocked state. During the listening state the port discards frames received from the attached network segment and it also discards frames switched from another port for forwarding. At this state, the port receives BPDUs from the network segment and directs them to the switch system module for processing. After 15 seconds, the switch port moves from the listening state to the learning state.

Learning State

A port changes to learning state after listening state. During the learning state, the port is listening for and processing BPDUs. In the listening state, the port begins to process user frames and start updating the MAC address table. But the user frames are not forwarded to the destination. After 15 seconds, the switch port moves from the learning state to the forwarding state.

Forwarding State

A port in the forwarding state forwards frames across the attached network segment. In a forwarding state, the port will process BPDUs, update its MAC Address table with frames that it receives, and forward user traffic through the port. Forwarding State is the normal state. Data and configuration messages are passed through the port, when it is in forwarding state.

Disabled State

A port in the disabled state does not participate in frame forwarding or the operation of STP because a port in the disabled state is considered non-operational.

5. What ports are blocking or forwarding?

The Switch Ports will go into a blocking state at the time of election process, when a switch receives a BPDU (bridge protocol data unit) on a port that indicates a better path to the Root Switch (Root Bridge), and if a port is not a Root port or a designated port.

A port in the forwarding state forwards frames across the attached network segment. In a forwarding state, the port will process BPDUs, update its MAC Address table with frames that it receives, and forward user traffic through the port. Forwarding State is the normal state. Data and configuration messages are passed through the port, when it is in forwarding state.

6. How it works if there are topology changes?

When a switch receives the topology change notification it will send a (TCA) topology change acknowledgement on its designated port towards the downstream switch. It will create a topology change notification itself and send it on its root port as well. When the Root Switch (Root Bridge) is aware that there is a topology change in the network, it starts to send out its Configuration BPDUs with the topology change (TC) bit set. Configuration BPDUs are received by every Switch (Bridge) in the network and all bridges become aware of the network topology change.

7. What is Broadcast Storm

When switches are interconnected for redundancy, a broadcast originating from a device connected to any switch, can cause the circulation of broadcasts around the network and can saturate the network consuming all available bandwidth. This network condition known as a broadcast storm. Broadcast storms consume entire bandwidth and deny bandwidth for normal network traffic.

Broadcast storm is a serious network problem and can shut down entire network in seconds.

Broadcast storms are prevented in networks using Spanning Tree Protocol.

8. How we calculate a loop-free path using spanning tree protocol.

All switch ports are in blocking mode to begin with. It takes approx. 30 seconds until packets can be forwarded.

> **Step 1:** Elect Root Bridge - Lowest bridge priority, if there is a tie then switch with lowest bridge ID

> **Step 2:** Elect Root Ports - Locate redundant paths to root bridge; block all but on root. Root Path Cost is cumulative cost of path to root bridge. Ports directly connected to Root Bridge will be root ports, otherwise lowest root path cost used.

> **Step 3:** Elect Designated Ports - Single port that sends and receives traffic from a switch to and from Root Bridge - Lowest cost path to Root Bridge.

9. What are the Spanning Tree Path Cost Values?

The Spanning Tree Cost Value is inversely proportional to the associated bandwidth of the path and therefore a path with a low-cost value is more preferable than a path with high cost value.

The following table lists the Port Cost value for different bandwidths.

Link Speed	Cost Value
10 Gbps	2
1Gbps	4
100 Mbps	19
10 Mbps	100

Table 1 Cost value

10. What is the STP selection Processes.?

When Booting: -

Election for Root Switch: -

- 1st switch will see the lowest priority value.
- Then Lowest Base Ethernet Mac address

1st check -

- Lowest cost of reached Root Switch.
- Lowest Sender Bridge-Id
- Lowest Port Priority (By Default 128)
- Lowest Port ID

Please Note important points: -

All the Port is by default designated port.

Root Port and Designated Port always in Forwarding State.

For Election of Designation Port: -

1st Check

- Lowest Path cost.
- Lowest Sender Bridge-Id.
- Lowest Priority 128.
- Lowest Port Id.

Please Note: -Non-Designate port is always in Blocking State.

By Default, Priority is 32768 for all switches.

STP States: -

- Disable – when the port is a shutdown stage.
- Listing – On Election from Root Port.

Designated port, blocking port will be Happen. Then switch will be listing BPDU Message receives from neighbor switch.

- After listing enter into learning stage

Switch will lean the Mac address. But it not forward data frames.

- Forwarding - It will be forward the data frames

11. What is the information content in the BPDU message? -

- Root ID (Root Switch Bridge ID)
- Sender Bridge ID
- STP Timer
- Root Path Cost

12. What is the Difference between Root Port and Designated Port?

The differences between Root Port and Designated Port are listed below.

1) Root Port is a single selected port on a Switch, other than Root Switch, with least Path Cost to reach the Root Bridge. The Designated Port is the port that has the lowest Spanning Tree Path Cost on a particular Local Area Network (LAN) segment.

2) The Root Port is the port on the Bridge (Switch) with the least Spanning Tree Path Cost from the switch to the Root Bridge. A Designated Port is the port on a Local Area Network (LAN) segment with the least Spanning Tree Path Cost to the Root Bridge (Root Switch).

3) There can be ONLY one Root Port on a Bridge (Switch). There may be multiple Designated Ports on a Bridge (Switch).

4) All the ports on a Root Bridge (Root Switch) are Designated Port and there is no Root Port on a Root Bridge (Root Switch).

5) A Root Port can NEVER be a Designated Port.

6) If one end of a Local Area Network (LAN) segment is a Designated Port, other end is called as Non-Designated Port (marked as NDP), if it is NOT a Root Port. Non-Designated Port will be always in Blocking State, to avoid Layer 2 Switching loops.

13. How Many Designated Ports Can Be Available on A Root Bridge?

All ports on a root bridge is designated ports.

14. How Many Root Bridges Can Be Available on A STP Configured Network?

If the priority value of the two switches are same, which switch would be elected as the root bridge
The switch with the lowest mac-address value would be elected as the root bridge

15. Is A Generic Ethernet Frame Modified When STP Is Configured on The Network?

STP is a protocol. It has its own frame when configured. So, it would not affect a generic ethernet frame on the network.

16. What Is Extended System Id?

The Extended System ID is utilized by spanning-tree to include the VLAN ID information inside 16-bit STP

17. Which command enhances the 802.1D convergence time on ports that are connected to hosts?

A. spanning-tree backbonefast

B. spanning-tree uplinkfast

C. spanning-tree portfast

D. spanning-tree cost512

Answer: C

Explanation

By using PortFast feature, the port won't spend 50 seconds to move from blocking (20sec), listening (15sec), learning (15sec) and finally forwarding but will jump directly to the forwarding state. This feature should be used on ports connected to hosts only because hosts surely don't send BPDU. An example of configuring PortFast on an interface is shown below:

SW(config)#interface FastEthernet0/1
SW(config-if)#spanning-tree portfast

18. **What is one benefit of PVST+?**

    A. PVST+ reduces the CPU cycles for all the switches in the network.

    B. PVST+ automatically selects the root bridge location, to provide optimization.

    C. PVST+ allows the root switch location to be optimized per vlan.

    D. PVST+ supports Layer 3 load balancing without loops

Answer: C

Explanation

Per VLAN Spanning Tree (PVST) maintains a spanning tree instance for each VLAN configured in the network. It means a switch can be the root bridge of a VLAN while another switch can be the root bridge of other VLANs in a common topology. For example, switch 1 can be the root bridge for Voice data while Switch 2 can be the root bridge for Video data. If designed correctly, it can optimize the network traffic.

19. **Which IEEE standard protocol is initiated as a result of successful DTP completion in a switch over Fast Ethernet?**

    A. 802.3ad

    B. 802.1w

    C. 802.1Q

    D. 802.1d

20. **Which port state is introduced by Rapid-PVST?**

    A. learning

    B. listening

    C. discarding

    D. forwarding

Answer: C

PVST+ is based on IEEE802.1D Spanning Tree Protocol (STP). But PVST+ has only 3 port states (discarding, learning and forwarding) while STP has 5 port states (blocking, listening, learning, forwarding and disabled). So discarding is a new port state in PVST+.

4.   TCP/IP

1.   Can you explain the architecture of TCP IP Protocol?

TCP/IP protocol maps four layers namely Application Layer, Transport and Internet Layer and Network Interface Layer.

Application Layer:

Accessibility of other services accessibility by applications is provided by the application layer. Protocol definitions that are used by application for exchanging data is also done by application layer. HTTP, FTP, SMTP, Telnet are some of the application layer protocols for exchanging information. Domain Name System, Routing Information Protocol, Simple Network Management Protocols are used for facilitating the use and management of TCP/IP networks.

Transport Layer:

Session and datagram communications services are provided by transport layer to the application layer. The protocols used for data transmission are TCP and UDP. TCP provides a reliable one-to-one communication service. Establishing TCP connection, sequencing and acknowledgement of sent packets are the responsibilities of TCP. UDP provides one-to-one, one-to-many, connectionless, unreliable communication services. UDP is recommended when the amount of data is small and fit into single packet.

The responsibilities of the OSI Transport layer and some of the responsibilities of OSI session layer are encompassed in the Transport layer.

Internet Layer

The responsibility of addressing, packaging, and routing functions are held by the Internet Layer. The protocols for this layer are IP, ARP, ICMP, and IGMP.

IP addressing, routing and fragmentation and assembling of packets are the responsibilities of IP protocol. Resolution of the Internet layer address to the network interface layer is the responsibility of ARP. Providing diagnostic functions and reporting errors due to the unsuccessful delivery of IP packets is dealt by ICMP. The management of IP multicast groups is the responsibility of IGMP.

Network Interface Layer

Placing TCP/IP packets on the medium of network and receiving TCP/IP packets off the network medium is the responsibility of Network Interface Layer. It was designed as independent of network access method, frame format, and medium. LAN technologies which use Ethernet and Token ring and WAN technologies such as x.25 are connected among them using Network Interface Layer.

2.   What layer in the TCP/IP stack is equivalent to the Transport layer of the OSI model?

- The TCP/IP protocol suite also known as a DARPA model

- It's a suite of protocol but gets its name because of the two more popular protocols TCP and IP
- There are four different layers in the TCP/IP reference model:
  1. Application
  2. Transport
  3. Internetwork
  4. Network Interface and Hardware

Where DOD model= TCP/IP. The following diagram shows the OSI Model, which is compared with TCP/IP Model and TCP/IP internet protocol suite.

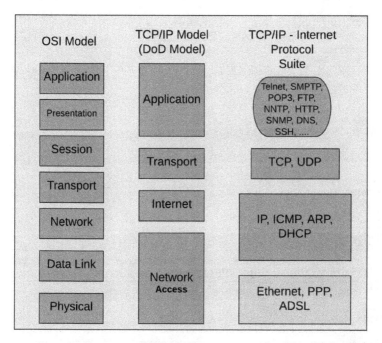

Figure 1 Comparing OSI Model with TCP/IP Model & Internet Protocol suite

Layer vise Comunication between the hosts is shows in the following snapshot.

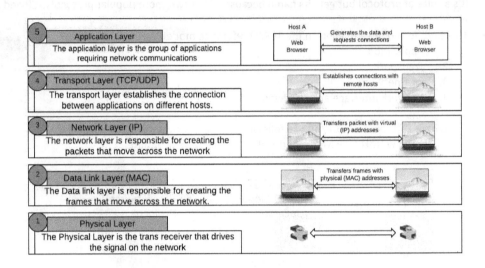

Figure 2 layer Diagram

The following figure shows the Comparison of TCP/IP with is OSI.

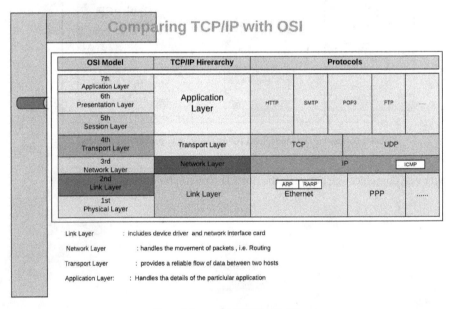

Figure 3 Comparing TCP/IP with OSI

3. **Which of the following describe the DHCP Discover message?**

- It uses FF:FF:FF:FF:FF:FF as a layer 2 broadcast.
- It uses UDP as the Transport layer protocol.
- It uses TCP as the Transport layer protocol.
- It does not use a layer 2 destination address.

A. 1 only
B. 1 and 2
C. 3 and 4
D. 4 only

Answer? Option B

Solution:

A client that sends out a DHCP Discover message in order to receive an IP address sends out a broadcast at both layer 2 and layer 3. The layer 2 broadcast is all Fs in hex, or FF:FF:FF:FF:FF:FF. The layer 3 broadcast is FF:FF:FF:FF:FF:FF, which means all networks and all hosts. DHCP is connectionless, which means it uses User Datagram Protocol (UDP) at the Transport layer, also called the Host-to-Host layer.

4. **You want to implement a mechanism that automates the IP configuration, including IP address, subnet mask, default gateway, and DNS information. Which protocol will you use to accomplish this?**

A. SMTP B. SNMP
C. DHCP D. ARP

Answer? Option c

Solution:

Dynamic Host Configuration Protocol (DHCP) is used to provide IP information to hosts on your network. DHCP can provide a lot of information, but the most common is IP address, subnet mask, default gateway, and DNS information.

5. **Which of the following is private IP address?**

A. 12.0.0.1 B. 168.172.19.39
C. 172.15.14.36 D. **192.168.24.43**

Solution:

Class A private address range is 10.0.0.0 through 10.255.255.255. Class B private address range is 172.16.0.0 through 172.31.255.255, and Class C private address range is 192.168.0.0 through 192.168.255.255.

6. **Explain how tracert, Ping, and TCP dump work and what they are used for?**
Ping is a command used to check the connectivity between source & destination. tracert is a command used to track the route followed by packet to reach towards destination & time required to reach the destination. TCP dump is a command line interface which is commonly used as a debugger for applications that generate or receive network traffic, or even the network setup itself.

7. **Explain how trace route work and what they are used for?**

Trace Route works by setting the TTL for a packet to 1, sending it towards the requested destination host, and listening for the reply. When the initiating machine receives a "time exceeded" response, it examines the packet to determine where the packet came from - this identifies the machine one hop away. Then the tracing machine generates a new packet with TTL 2 and uses the response to determine the machine 2 hops away, and so on.

- Maximum TTL =255
- Trace route is based on UDP protocol, it sends UDP packets
- reply come as ICMP TTL exceed message

  http://ccieblog.co.uk/basic-troubleshooting-commands/how-does-traceroute-work

8. What are Common Port numbers?

The common port is shown in the following table

TCP		UDP	
Telnet	23	SNMP	161
SMTP	25	TFTP	69
HTTP	80	DNS	53
FTP	21		
DNS	53		
HTTPS	443		

Table 2 Common Ports

Internet Layer Protocol Field in IP Header	
Protocol	Protocol Number
ICMP	1
IP in IP (tunneling)	4
IGRP	9
EIGRP	88
OSPF	89
IPv6	41
GRE	47
Layer 2 tunnel (L2TP)	115

Table 3 Internet Layer Protocol field IP Header

9. Can you explain TCP header in detail?

The following figure show the information of TCP Header.

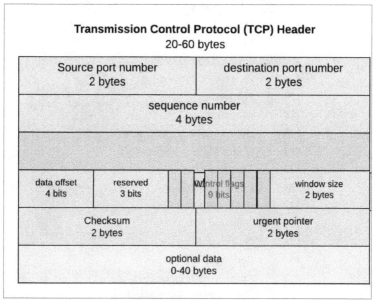

Figure 4 TCP Header

- Source Port: 16 bits: It's the source port number.
- Destination Port: 16 bits: It's the destination port number.
- Sequence Number: 32 bits: The sequence number of the first data octet in this segment (except when SYN is present). If SYN is present the sequence number is the initial sequence number (ISN) and the first data octet is ISN+1.
- Acknowledgment Number: 32 bits if the ACK control bit is set this field contains the value of the next sequence number the sender of the segment is expecting to receive. Once a connection is established this is always sent.
- Size of TCP header is 32+ bits because source port and destination ports are 16 bit each. The length of the data section is not specified in the TCP segment header. It can be calculated by subtracting the combined length of the TCP header and the encapsulating IP header from the total IP datagram length

10. Can you explain ICMP protocol?
- ICMP is a protocol within the TCP/IP stack
- Provide control, troubleshooting, and error messages.
- It runs over IP, like TCP and UDP do, but is a network-layer protocol, like IP, rather than a transport layer protocol like TCP and UDP are.
- RFC 792 defines ICMP, which provides routing, diagnostic and error functionality for IP.
- Although ICMP messages are encapsulated within IP datagrams, ICMP processing is considered to be (and is typically implemented as) part of the IP layer.

ICMP packets have the following characteristics:
- They can provide hosts with information about network problems.
- They are encapsulated within IP datagrams.

Important ICMP messages are as follows

Type	Meaning
1	Destination Unreachable
2	Packet Too Big
3	Time Exceeded
4	Parameter Problem
128	Echo Request
129	Echo Reply
103	Group Membership Query
131	Group Membership Report
132	Group Membership Reduction
133	Router Solicitation
134	Router Advertisement
135	Neighbor Solicitation
136	Neighbor Advertisement
137	Redirect
138	Router Renumbering

Table 4 ICMP messages

11. Can you explain IP protocol?

The Internet Protocol (IP) is the method or protocol by which data is sent from one computer to another on the Internet. Each computer (known as a host) on the Internet has at least one IP address that uniquely identifies it from all other computers on the Internet.

12. Can you explain the concept of DHCP? How does DHCP work? How can we configure DHCP?

DHCP (Dynamic Host Configuration Protocol) is a protocol that is commonly used in networks for dynamic IP addressing configuration. Every user's device needs at least IP address to join the network and connect to services.

a. Host connecting to network (cable or wireless) sends DHCP discover message to all hosts in Layer 2 segment (destination address is FF:FF:FF:FF:FF:FF). Frame with this DISCOVER message hits the DHCP Server.

b. After the DHCP Server receives discover message it suggests the IP addressing offering to the client host by unicast.
This OFFER message contains:
- proposed IP address for client (here 192.168.1.10)
- subnet mask to identify the subnet space (here 255.255.255.0)
- IP of default gateway for subnet (here 192.168.1.1)
- IP of DNS server for name translations (here 8.8.8.8)

Now after the client receives the offer it requests the information officially sending REQUEST message to server this time by unicast.

Server sends ACKNOWLEDGE message confirming the DHCP lease to client. Now client is allowed to use new IP settings.

13. Explain the ARP packet header?

The following figure show the information of ARP header.

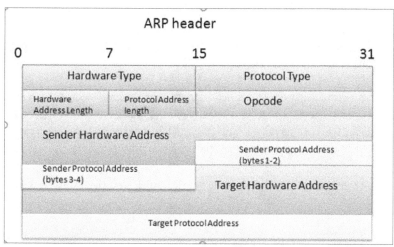

Figure 5 ARP Header

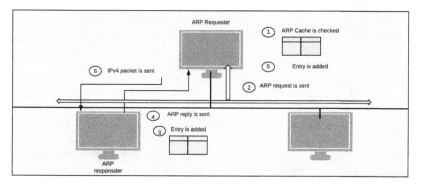

Figure 6 ARP Request

- The ARP protocols perform the translation between IP addresses to MAC addresses
- It works on Layer 2
- ARP request is broadcast where ARP reply is always unicast
- that is how a switch creates its mac-table
- ARP spoofing attack can happen by populating falsified MAC addresses

14. What is RARP (Reverse Address Resolution Protocol)? How does it work?

perform the translation between MAC addresses to IP addresses to learn its own IP address upon booting up for the first time

Is a protocol by which a physical machine in a local area network can **request to learn its IP address from a gateway server's Address Resolution Protocol (ARP)** table or cache when it first boots up?

29

A network administrator creates a table in a local area networks gateway router that maps the physical machine (or Media Access Control - MAC address) addresses to corresponding Internet Protocol addresses.

When a new machine is set up, its RARP client program requests from the RARP server on the router to be sent its IP address. Assuming that an entry has been set up in the router table, the RARP server will return the IP address to the machine which can store it for future use. The following diagram show the working of the RARP.

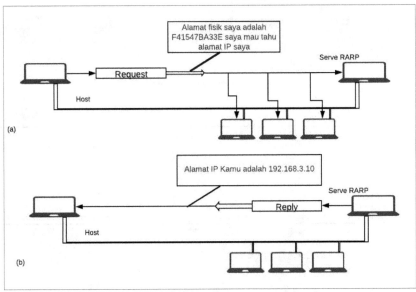

Figure 7 RARP Work

15. What are the different fields in the IPv4 Packet Header?

The following diagram show the different fields in the IPV4 Packet Header.

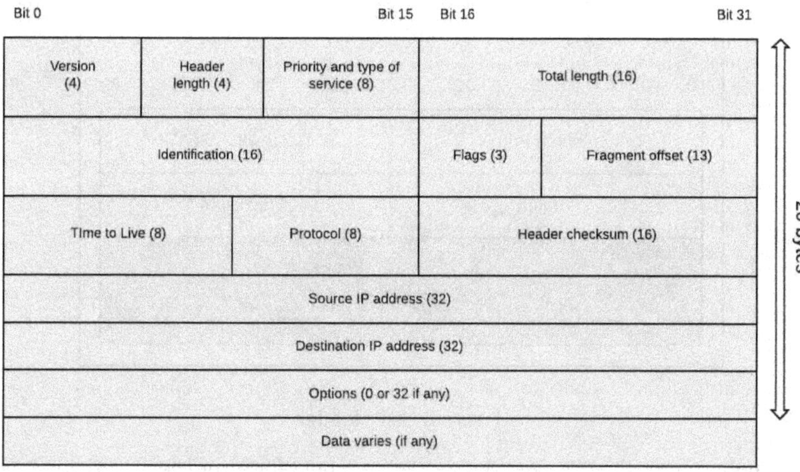

Bit 0
Bit 15
Bit 16
Bit 31
Version (4)
Header length (4)
Priority and type of service (8)
Total length (16)
Identification (16)
Flags (3)
Fragment offset (13)
Time to Live (8)
Protocol (8)
Header checksum (16)
Source IP address (32)
Destination IP address (32)
Options (0 or 32 if any)
Data varies (if any)
20 bytes

Figure 8 IP Header

The following figure show the comparison between IPV4 & IPV6

IPv4 & IPv6 Header Comparision
IPv4 Header
Version
IHL
Types of Service
Total Length
Identification
Flags
Fragment Offset
Time to Live
Protocol
Header Checksum
Source Address
Destination Address
Options
Padding
IPv6 Header
Version
Traffic Class
Flow Label
Payload Length
Next Header
Hop Limit
Source Address
Destination Address
Legend
- field's name kept from IPV4 to IPv6
- field's not kept in IPv6
- Name & position changed in IPv6
- New field in IPv6

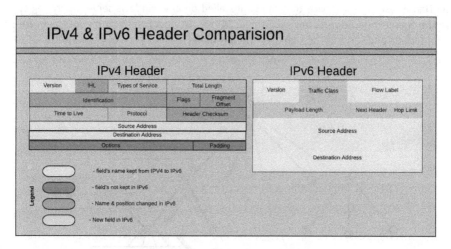

Figure 9 IPV4 and IPV6 Header Comparison

16. What is included in n the UDP Packet?

The figure shows the information about UDP Header.

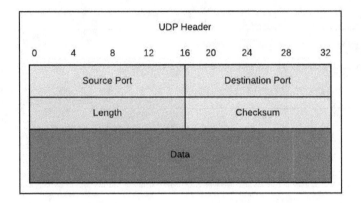

Figure 8 UDP Header

It has source port and destination port and a checksum field for error checking Layer 4 protocol for encapsulating data and its unreliable and connection less.

17. What is DNS?

Domain Name System is a service that can be installed on any windows server operating system to resolve the Name to IP Address and vice-versa. TCP/IP networks, such as the Internet, use DNS to locate computers and services through user-friendly name

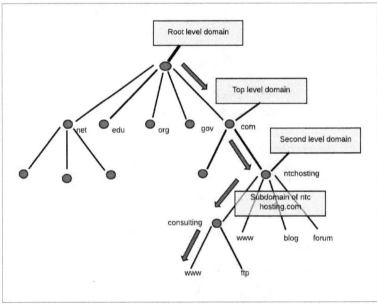

Figure 10 Level Domains

The following diagram show the DNS Header format.

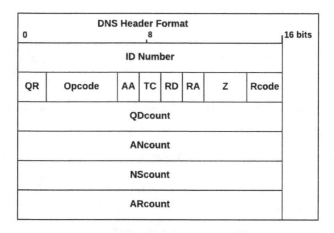

Figure 11 DNS Header Format

1) Translates Domain Name into IP Address
2) DNS primarily uses User Datagram Protocol (UDP) on port number 53 to serve requests.[3]
3) DNS queries consist of a single UDP request from the client followed by a single UDP reply from the server.
4) The Transmission Control Protocol (TCP) is used when the response data size exceeds 512 bytes

5) The DNS is a hierarchical distributed naming system for computers, services, or any resource connected to the Internet or a private network.

   - top level domains have .ca .pk .us type of address
   - second-level domain like .com .net
   - sub-domains examples can be wichita.edu, kind of an organizational level DNS

6) DNS implements a distributed database to store this name and address information for all public hosts on the Internet.
7) it translates the domain name into the IP address
8) configuration of primary, secondary, and tertiary DNS servers is possible
9) There are security concerns also while using DNS reverse lookups are also possible:
   request sent with an IP address to get the domain name, DNS additionally includes support for caching requests and for redundancy.

18. What is the main purpose of a DNS server?

DNS servers are used to resolve FQDN hostnames into IP addresses and vice versa.

19. What is the port no of DNS?

Port no 53.

20. What is a Forward Lookup?

Resolving Host Names to IP Addresses.

21. What is Reverse Lookup?

It's a file contains host names to IP mapping information.

22. What is a Resource Record?

It is a record provides the information about the resources available in the N/W infrastructure.

23. What are the diff. DNS Roles?

Standard Primary, Standard Secondary, & AD Integrated.

24. What is a Zone?

Zone is a sub tree of DNS database.

25. What is primary, Secondary, stub & AD Integrated Zone?

- **Primary Zone:** - zone which is saved as normal text file with filename (.dns) in DBS folder. Maintains a read, write copy of zone database.
- **Secondary Zone:** - maintains a read only copy of zone database on another DNS server. Provides fault tolerance and load balancing by acting as backup server to primary server.
- **Stub zone:** - contains a copy of name server and SOA records used for reducing the DNS search orders. Provides fault tolerance and load balancing.

26. How do you manually create SRV records in DNS?

This is on windows server go to run ---> dnsmgmt.msc right click on the zone you want to add srv record to and choose "other new record" and choose service location(srv).

27. What is the main purpose of SRV records?

SRV records are used in locating hosts that provide certain network services.

28. What Is DDNS?

Dynamic DNS or DDNS is a method of updating, in real time, a Domain Name System to point to a changing IP address on the Internet. This is used to provide a persistent domain name for a resource that may change location on the network.

29. How does ping work?

The ping command first sends an echo request packet to an address, and then waits for a reply. The ping is successful only if:

the echo request gets to the destination, and the destination is able to get an echo reply back to the source within a predetermined time called a timeout. The default value of this timeout is two seconds on Cisco routers. The following diagram show the working of ping.

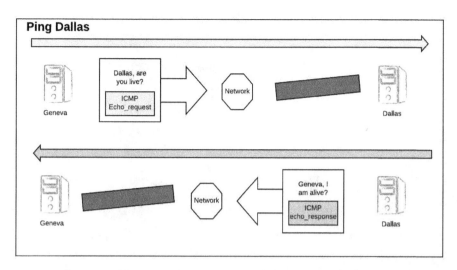

Figure 12 Ping Dallas

For more information the following diagram shows the PING expiation with TTL field

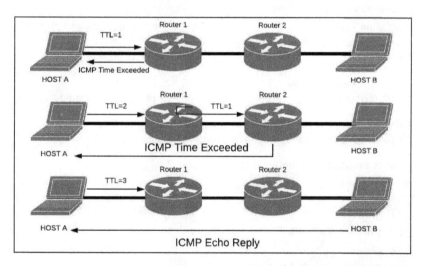

Figure 13 PING explanation with TTL field

30. How does the packet route on L2?

- on L2, mac-table is used to route packet
- In Layer 2 switching happens on mac-address to port mapping
- mac-table contains entry with mac-address to physical ports
  A switch checks the destination mac-address and match it with mac-table to send it
  to the port

you can further explain how mac-table and routing tables are build

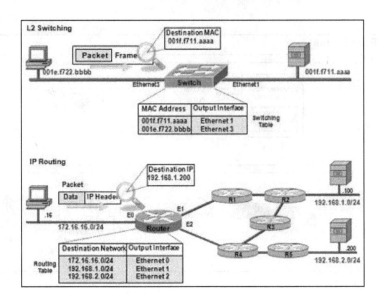

Figure 14 Mac-table and routing tables

31. How does the packet route on L3?

while on Layer 3 we have routing table which have IP address and physical port mapping router checks destination IP address and check routing table for the same IP address and if found send it to the associated port on L3, RIB or routing table is used to route the packet

L2 Switch can only route traffic by the Layer 2 header (MAC)
L3 Switch can route packets by the Layer 3 header (IP) and off course L2 as well.

If you only have a L2 device, you will need a L3 device to route traffic between VLANs either a L3 switch or a router configure as a router on a stick.

32. How does a packet route between two computers?

There are 2 ways either via L2 or via L3
You can further explain how mac-table and routing tables are build
can't find anything precise
it's a very generic question, it can have so many things in it

33. How ICMP packet handled by NAT?

For TCP and UDP NAT usually works with IP address and port combination but in ICMP we don't have any port numbers, there is one random number selected by ICMP NAT uses that random number and IP address to make translation that random number is called query ID
* For ICMP query/reply type messages like Echoes (pings), NAPT uses the ICMP Query ID (sometimes just called the ICMP ID) the same way it would use a TCP or UDP port number.
* SO basically, ICMP query ID is used for ICMP over NAT

34. If I am unable to send a packet between two computers how will you troubleshoot it?

* By making sure It's Actually Your Network Problem
* Power Cycle Everything and Check Other Devices
* Check Physical Connections
* Run the Windows Network Troubleshooter

- Check for a Valid IP Address
- Try a Ping and Trace Its Route
- Contact Your ISP

35. Why is OSI model layered?

- A reference model is a conceptual blueprint of how communications should take place.
- It addresses all the processes required for effective communication and divides these processes into logical groupings called layers.
- When a communication system is designed in this manner, it's known as layered architecture.
- It provides a structural approach to troubleshoot an issue.

36. What is difference between TCP/IP and UDP?

- TCP is connection-oriented protocol
- UDP is Connectionless Protocol

1) **TCP** (Transmission Control Protocol). TCP is a connection-oriented protocol, a connection can be made from client to server, and from then on, any data can be sent along that connection.
   a. **Reliable** - when you send a message along a TCP socket, you know it will get there unless the connection fails completely. If it gets lost along the way, the server will re-request the lost part. This means complete integrity; things don't get corrupted.
   b. **Ordered** - if you send two messages along a connection, one after the other, you know the first message will get there first. You don't have to worry about data arriving in the wrong order.
   c. **Heavyweight** - when the low level parts of the TCP "stream" arrive in the wrong order, resend requests have to be sent, and all the out of sequence parts have to be put back together, so requires a bit of work to piece together.
2) **UDP** (User Datagram Protocol). A simpler message-based connectionless protocol. With UDP you send messages (packets) across the network in chunks.

   a. **Unreliable** - When you send a message, you don't know if it'll get there, it could get lost on the way.
   b. **Not ordered** - If you send two messages out, you don't know what order they'll arrive in.
   c. **Lightweight** - No ordering of messages, no tracking connections, etc. It's just fire and forget! This means it's a lot quicker, and the network card / OS have to do very little work to translate the data back from the packets.

The following table shows the summary comparison of UDP and TCP

Summary Comparison of UDP and TCP		
Characteristic / Description	UDP	TCP
General Description	Simple, high-speed low-functionality rapper that interfaces applications to the network layer and does idle else.	Full-featured protocol that allows applications to send data reliably without worrying about network layer issues.
Protocol Connection Setup	Connectionless; data is sent without setup	Connection-oriented; connection must be established prior to transmission.
Data Interface to Application	Message-based: data is sent in discrete packages by the application.	Stream-based: data is sent by the application with no particular structure.
Reliability and Acknowledgments	Unreliable, best-effort delivery without acknowledgments.	Reliable delivery of messages; all data is acknowledged.
Retransmissions	Not performed. Application must detect lost data and retransmit if needed.	Delivery of al data is managed. and lost data is retransmitted automatically.
Features Provided to Manage Flow of Data	None	Flow control using sliding windows; window size adjustment heuristics; congestion avoidance algorithms.
Overhead	Very low	Low, but higher than UDP
Transmission Speed	Very High	High, but not as high as UDP
Data Quantity Suitability	Small to moderate amounts of data (up to a few hundred bytes)	Small to very large amounts of data (up to gigabytes)
Types of Application that use the protocol	Applications where data delivery speed matters more than completeness, where	Most protocols and applications sending data that must be

Table 5 Comparison of UDP and TCP

37. Explain 3-way handshake of TCP

The TCP three-way handshake in Transmission Control Protocol (also called the TCP-handshake; three message handshake and/or SYN-SYN-ACK) is the method used by TCP set up a TCP/IP connection over an Internet Protocol based network.

This 3-way handshake process is also designed so that both ends can initiate and negotiate separate TCP socket connections at the same time.

- **SYN**chronize and **ACK**nowledge messages are indicated by a either the SYN bit, or the ACK bit inside the TCP header,

- And the **SYN-ACK message** has both the SYN and the ACK bits turned on (set to 1) in the TCP header.

UDP does not perform this 3-way handshake and for this reason, it is referred to as an unreliable protocol.

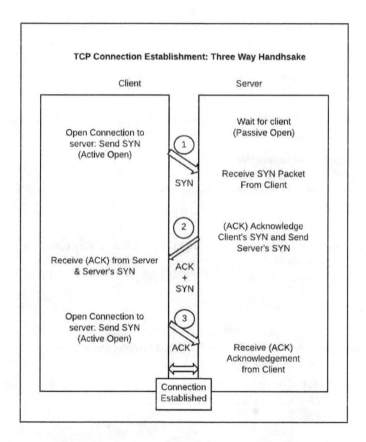

Figure 15 TCP Connection Establishment 3-Way Handshake

38. Two users are accessing a Network application simultaneously. Which fields in the TCP/IP header would the server use to distinguish between the connections?

a. Source IP address in the IP header.

b. Destination IP address in the IP header.

c. Source port in the TCP header.

d. Destination port in the TCP header.

Answer c

39. **A web client opens two instances of a website using a browser. Which of the fields would be different for both the connections?**

    a. Source port number.

    b. Destination port number.

    c. Source IP address

    d. Destination IP address.

Answer a

40. **Which of the following fields are used to identify if the packet has to be sent on the same or different network?**

    a. Destination port number.

    b. Subnet Mask.

    c. Destination network address.

    d. Domain name of the destination.

Answer b

41. **A PC does not have DNS server IP address configured on its adapter. What would happen if the user pings a website on the PC?**

    a. Response would be received as ping uses ICMP.

    b. Response would be received as ping does not use DNS.

    c. Response would fail as DNS resolution would fail.

    d. None of the above.

Answer c

42. **Which field is used in a TCP/IP header is used to identify the server application?**

    a. Source port number

    b. Destination port number.

    c. Socket number.

    d. Socket port number.

Answer b

43. **When does data transfer commence in a TCP based communication?**

    a. After the TCP 3-way handshake

    b. Before the TCP 3-way handshake

    c. After the TCP 4-way handshake

    d. None of the above.

Answer a

44. **When does the TCP 4-way handshake commence?**

    a. There is nothing like TCP 4-way handshake.

    b. After the 3-way handshake

    c. Before the 4-way handshake

    d. After data transfer is completed.

Answer d

45. Where is the source port number used in a TCP/IP header?

    a. Inside transport layer headers like TCP or UDP

    b. Inside IP layer header.

    c. Inside application layer headers like FTP, HTTP etc.

    d. None of the above

Answer a

46. What does the command "IP name-server 255.255.255.255" accomplish?

    a. It sets the domain name lookup to be a local broadcast.

    b. This is an illegal command.

    c. It disables domain name lookup.

    d. The command is now defunct and has been replaced by "IP server-name IP any"

Answer: a

By default, DNS is enabled on a router with a server address of 255.255.255.255, which provides for
a local broadcast.

5. IPV6

1. **Which of these statements best describes the major difference between an IPv4-compatible tunnel and a 6to4 tunnel?**

    A. An IPv4-compatible tunnel is a static tunnel, but a 6to4 tunnel is a semiautomatic tunnel.
    B. The deployment of an IPv4-compatible tunnel requires a special code on the edge routers, but a 6to4 tunnel does not require any special code.
    C. An IPv4-compatible tunnel is typically used only between two IPv6 domains, but a 6to4 tunnel is used to connect two or more IPv6 domains.
    D. For an IPv4-compatible tunnel, the ISP assigns only IPv4 addresses for each domain, but for a 6to4 tunnel, the ISP assigns only IPv6 addresses for each domain.

    Answer C

2. **Which IPv6 address would you ping to determine if OSPFv3 is able to send and receive unicast packets across a link?**

    A. anycast address
    B. site-local multicast
    C. global address of the link
    D. unique local address
    E. link-local address

    Answer? E

3. **You are using IPv6 and would like to configure EIGRPv3. Which three of these correctly describe how you can perform this configuration? (Choose three)**

    A. EIGRP for IPv6 is directly configured on the interfaces over which it runs.
    B. EIGRP for IPv6 is not configured on the interfaces over which it runs, but if a user uses passive-interface configuration, EIGRP for IPv6 needs to be configured on the interface that is made passive.
    C. There is a network statement configuration in EIGRP for IPv6, the same as for IPv4.
    D. There is no network statement configuration in EIGRP for IPv6.
    E. When a user uses a passive-interface configuration, EIGRP for IPv6 does not need to be configured on the interface that is made passive.
    F. When a user uses a non-passive-interface configuration, EIGRP for IPv6 does not need to be configured on the interface that is made passive

    Answer? AEF

4. **Which of these statements accurately identifies how Unicast Reverse Path Forwarding can be employed to prevent the use of malformed or forged IP sources addresses?**

    A. It is applied only on the input interface of a router.
    B. If is applied only on the output interface of a router.
    C. It can be configured either on the input or output interface of a router.
    D. It cannot be configured on a router interface.
    E. It is configured under any routing protocol process.

Answer: A

5. **Unicast Reverse Path Forwarding can perform all of these actions except which one?**

   A. Examine all packets received to make sure that the source addresses and source interfaces appear in the routing table and match the interfaces where the packets were received
   B. Check to see if any packet received at a router interface arrives on the best return path
   C. combine with a configured ACL
   D. Log its events, if you specify the logging options for the ACL entries used by the unicast RPF command
   E. Inspect IP packets encapsulated in tunnels, such as GRE

   Answer: E

6. **During the IPv6 address resolution, a node sends a neighbor solicitation message in order to discover which of these?**

   A. The Layer 2 multicast address of the destination node
   B. The solicited node multicast address of the destination node
   C. The Layer 2 address of the destination node based on the destination IPv6 address
   D. The IPv6 address of the destination node based on the destination Layer 2 address

   Answer: C

7. **When using IP SLA FTP operation, which two FTP modes are supported? (Choose two)**

   A. Only the FTP PUT operation type is supported.
   B. Active mode is supported.
   C. Passive FTP transfer modes are supported.
   D. FTP URL specified for the FTP GET operation is not supported.

   Answer: B C

8. **As a CCNA candidate, you must have a firm understanding of the IPv6 address structure. Refer to IPv6 address, could you tell me how many bits are included in each filed?**
   A. 24
   B. 4
   C. 3
   D. 16
   Answer: D

   Explanation: The format of An IPv6 address is X:X:X:X:X:X:X:X where X is a 16-bit hexadecimal field. For example: 110A:0192:190F:0000:0000:082C:875A:132c

9. **In practical IPv6 application, a technology encapsulates IPv6 packets inside IPv4 packets, this technology is called what?**

   A. tunneling
   B. hashing

C. routing
D. NAT

Answer: A

10. Internet Protocol version 6 (IPv6) is the next-generation Internet Protocol version designated as the successor to IPv4 because IPv4 address space is being exhausted. Which one of the following descriptions about IPv6 is correct?

A. Addresses are not hierarchical and are assigned at random.
B. Broadcasts have been eliminated and replaced with multicasts.
C. There are 2.7 billion available addresses.
D. An interface can only be configured with one IPv6 address.

Answer: B

11. Which two of these statements are true of IPv6 address representation? (Choose two)

A. The first 64 bits represent the dynamically created interface ID.
B. A single interface may be assigned multiple IPV6 addresses of any type.
C. Every IPV6 interface contains at least one loopback address.
D. Leading zeros in an IPV6 16-bit hexadecimal field are mandatory.

Answer: B C

Explanation: Leading zeros in IPv6 are optional do that 05C7 equals 5C7 and 0000 equals 0 -> D is not correct.

12. Which three of the following are IPv6 transition mechanisms? (Choose three)

A. 6to4 tunneling
B. GRE tunneling
C. ISATAP tunneling
D. Teredo tunneling
E. VPN tunneling
F. PPP tunneling

Answer: A C D

Explanation: Below is a summary of IPv6 transition technologies:

6 to 4 tunneling: This mechanism allows IPv6 sites to communicate with each other over the IPv4 network without explicit tunnel setup. The main advantage of this technology is that it requires no end-node reconfiguration and minimal router configuration but it is not intended as a permanent solution.

ISATAP tunneling (Intra-Site Automatic Tunnel Addressing Protocol): is a mechanism for transmitting IPv6 packets over IPv4 network. The word "automatic" means that once an ISATAP server/router has been set up, only the clients must be configured to connect to it.

Teredo tunneling: This mechanism tunnels IPv6 datagrams within IPv4 UDP datagrams, allowing private IPv4 address and IPv4 NAT traversal to be used.

In fact, GRE tunneling is also a IPv6 transition mechanism but is not mentioned in CCNA so we shouldn't choose it (there are 4 types of IPv6 transition mechanisms mentioned in CCNA; they are: manual, 6-to-4, Teredo and ISATAP).

13. Which two descriptions are correct about characteristics of IPv6 unicast addressing? (Choose two)

    A. Global addresses start with 2000::/3.
    B. Link-local addresses start with FF00::/10.
    C. Link-local addresses start with FE00:/12.
    D. There is only one loopback address and it is ::1.

Answer: A D
Explanation:

Below is the list of common kinds of IPv6 addresses:

Loopback address	::1
Link-local address	FE80::/10
Site-local address	FEC0::/10
Global address	2000::/3
Multicast address	FF00::/8

14. Select the valid IPv6 addresses. (Choose all apply)

    A. ::192:168:0:1
    B. 2002:c0a8:101::42
    C. 2003:dead:beef:4dad:23:46:bb:101
    D. ::
    E. 2000::
    F. 2001:3452:4952:2837::

Answer: A B C D F

Explanation:

Answers A B C are correct because A and B are the short form of 0:0:0:0:192:168:0:1 and 2002:c0a8:0101:0:0:0:0:0042 while C is normal IPv6 address.

Answer D is correct because "::" is named the "unspecified" address and is typically used in the source field of a datagram that is sent by a device that seeks to have its IP address configured.

Answer E is not correct because a global-unicast IPv6 address is started with binary 001, denoted as 2000::/3 in IPv6 and it also known as an aggregatable global unicast address. The 2000:: (in particular, 2000::/3) is just a prefix and is not a valid IPv6 address.

The entire global-unicast IPv6 address range is from 2000::/128 to 3FFF:FFFF:FFFF:FFFF:FFFF:FFFF:FFFF/128, resulting in a total usable space of over 42,535,295,865,117,307,932,921,825,928,971,000,000 addresses, which is only 1/8th of the entire IPv6 address space!

15. Which two reductions are the correct reductions of the IPv6 address 2001:0d02:0000:0000:0014:0000:0000:0095? (Choose two)

A. 2001:0d02:::0014:::0095
B. 2001:d02::14::95
C. 2001:d02:0:0:14::95
D. 2001:d02::14:0:0:95

Answer: C D

Explanation

A is not correct because we can't use triple colons (:::) in IPv6 presentation. B is not correct because we can't use double colons (::) twice. You can use it only once in any address because if two double colons are placed in the same address, there will be no way to identify the size of each block of 0s. Remember the following techniques to shorten an IPv6 address:

- Omit leading 0s in the address field, so: 0000 can be compressed to just: 0 and: 0d02 can be com-
Pressed to: d02 (but: 1d00 cannot be compressed to: 1d)

- Use double colons (::), but just once, to represent a contiguous block of 0s, so 2001:0d02:0000:0000:0014:0000:0000:0095 can be compressed to 2001:0d02:: 14:0:0:95 or 2001:0d02:0:0:14:: 95

16. What is the IPv6 address FF02::2 used for?

A. all hosts in a local segment
B. all routers in a local segment
C. all hosts in a particular Multicast group
D. all routers in an autonomous system

Answer: B

Explanation: Below lists some reserved and well-known IPv6 multicast address in the reserved multicast address range (FF00:: to FF0F::)

Multicast Address   Multicast Group
FF01::1 All IPv6 nodes within the node-local scope
FF01::2 All IPv6 routers within the node-local scope
FF02::1 All IPv6 nodes within the link-local scope
FF02::2 All IPv6 routers within the link-local scope
FF02::5 All OSPFv3 routers within the link-local scope
FF02::6 All OSPFv3 designated routers within the link-local scope

FF02::9 All RIPng routers within the link-local scope
FF02::A All EIGRP routers within the link-local scope
FF02::D All PIM routers within the link-local scope
FF02::1:2   All DHCPv6 agents (servers and relays) within the link-local scope
FF05::2 All IPv6 routers within the site-local scope
FF02::1:FF00:0/104   IPv6 solicited-node multicast address within the link-local scope

17. **Refer to the exhibit. Routers R1 and R2 are IPv6 BGP peers that have been configured to support a neighbor relationship over an IPv4 internetwork. Which three neighbor IP addresses are valid choices to use in the highlighted section of the exhibit? (Choose three)**

    A. ::0A43:0002
    B. 0A43:0002::
    C. ::10.67.0.2
    D. 10.67.0.2::
    E. 0:0:0:0:0:0:10.67.0.2
    F. 10.67.0.2:0:0:0:0:0:0

Answer: A C E

Explanation

The automatic tunneling mechanism uses a special type of IPv6 address, termed an "IPv4-compatible" address. An IPv4-compatible address is identified by an all-zeros 96-bit prefix and holds an IPv4 address in the low-order 32-bits. IPv4-compatible addresses are structured as follows:

Therefore, an IPv4 address of 10.67.0.2 will be written as ::10.67.0.2 or 0:0:0:0:0:0:10.67.0.2 or ::0A43:0002 (with 10[decimal] = 0A[hexa] ; 67[decimal] = 43[hexa] ; 0[hexa] = 0[decimal] ; 2[hexa] = 2[decimal])

18. **Refer to the exhibit. The 6to4 overlay tunnel configuration has been applied on each router to join isolated IPv6 networks over a IPv4 network. Which statements regarding the 6to4 overlay tunnel is true?**

    A. The least significant 32 bits in the address referenced by the ipv6 route 2002::/16 Tunnel0 command will correspond to the interface E0/0 IPv4 address
    B. The least significant 32 bits in the address referenced by the ipv6 route 2002::/16 Tunnel0 command will correspond to the IPv4 address assigned to the tunnel source
    C. The configuration is invalid since the tunnel source command must be configured with an IPv6 address
    D. This is actually a configuration example of an IPv4-compatible tunnel and not a 6to4 tunnel
    E. This is actually a configuration example of an ISATAP overlay tunnel and not a 6to4 tunnel

Answer: B

Explanation

6to4 tunnels use IPv6 addresses that concatenate 2002::/16 with the 32-bit IPv4 address of the edge router, creating a 48-bit prefix. The tunnel interface on R1 has an IPv6 prefix of 2002:4065:4001:1::/64, where 4065:4001 is the hexadecimal equivalent of 64.101.64.1, the IPv4 address of its interface in the IPv4 network. The tunnel interface on R2 has an IPv6 prefix of

2002:4065:4101:1::/64, where 4065:4101 is the hexadecimal equivalent of 64.101.65.1, the IPv4 address of its interface in the IPv4 network.

When R1 receives a packet with IPv6 destination address of 2002:4065:4101:1:: (from the left IPv6 network, for example) R1 will:

- Take the IPv6 destination address of that packet (2002:4065:4101:1::) and convert it into an IPv4 address. In this case, the IPv4 address is 40.65.41.01 in hexa, which is 64.101.65.1 in decimal format.
- R1 encapsulates the IPv6 packet in an IPv4 packet with a destination address of 64.101.65.1; the packet is routed normally through the IPv4 network to R2
- R2 receives the IPv4 packet, decapsulates and routes it normally to its final IPv6 destination.

19. **What will occur when an IPv6 enabled router running 6to4 must transmit a packet to a remote destination and the next hop is the address of 2002::/16 ?**

A. The IPv6 packet has its header removed and replaced with an IPv4 header
B. The IPv6 packet is encapsulated in an IPv4 packet using an IPv4 protocol type of 41
C. The IPv6 packet is dropped because that destination is unable to route IPv6 packets
D. The packet is tagged with an IPv6 header and the IPv6 prefix is included

Answer: B

20. **What are three IPv6 transition mechanisms? (Choose three)**

A. 6to4 tunneling
B. VPN tunneling
C. GRE tunneling
D. ISATAP tunneling
E. PPP tunneling
F. Teredo tunneling

Answer: A D F

Explanation

Below is a summary of IPv6 transition technologies:

6 to 4 tunneling: This mechanism allows IPv6 sites to communicate with each other over the IPv4 network without explicit tunnel setup. The main advantage of this technology is that it requires no end-node reconfiguration and minimal router configuration but it is not intended as a permanent solution.

ISATAP tunneling (Intra-Site Automatic Tunnel Addressing Protocol): is a mechanism for transmitting IPv6 packets over IPv4 network. The word "automatic" means that once an ISATAP server/router has been set up, only the clients must be configured to connect to it.

Teredo tunneling: This mechanism tunnels IPv6 datagrams within IPv4 UDP datagrams, allowing private IPv4 address and IPv4 NAT traversal to be used.

In fact, GRE tunneling is also a IPv6 transition mechanism but is not mentioned in ROUTE so we shouldn't choose it (there are 4 types of IPv6 transition mechanisms mentioned in ROUTE; they are: manual, 6-to-4, Teredo and ISATAP).

6.   ROUTING INFORMATION PROTOCOL (RIP)

1. **What is the destination IP address of a Rip v1 packet?**

   Rip v1 is a broadcast packet. The destination IP address of a Rip v1 packet is 255.255.255.255

2. **What is the main difference in RIP v1 and v2 packet?**

   RIP v1 does not include the subnet mask information inside the packet. It does not support classless addressing. RIP v2 includes the subnet mask information inside the packet. For example, assume that the sub netted network 192.168.1.64/26 is configured on a RIP enabled router. If RIP v1 is configured, the route would be advertised as 192.168.1.0 (It would take the default subnet mask of /24 and not /26). If RIP v2 is configured, the subnet mask information (/26) would also be advertised in the route.

3. **What is the major benefit of dynamic routing protocol like RIP over Static route?**

   In a static route, the route entries have to be manually configured on the router; whereas in a dynamic routing protocol like Rip, routes are learnt automatically.

4. **Can a subnet mask information be stored in a Rip v1 packet?**

   Rip v1 is a classful routing protocol. It does not understand classless concepts like Subnets. So, it is not possible.

5. **What is the multicast address that Rip v2 uses?**

   224.0.0.9

6. **Which transport layer protocol does RIP use and the associated port number?**

   UDP – Port 520

7. **What is the administrative distance of RIPip?**

   120

8. **Which protocol should you select if the network diameter is more than 17 hops?**

   a) RIPv1

   b) RIPv2

   c) EIGRP

   d) Both RIPv1 and RIPv2

   Answer: a

   Explanation: RIP v1 has network diameter is more than 17 hopes.

9. **Which command displays RIP routing updates?**

   a) Show IP route

   b) Debug IP rip

   c) Show protocols

   d) Debug IP route

Answer: b

Explanation: The debug IP rip command is used to show the Internet Protocol (IP) Routing Information Protocol (RIP) updates being sent and received on the router.

10. **Which protocol gives a full route table update every 30 seconds?**

    a) IEGRP

    b) RIP

    c) both IEGRP and RIP

    d) none of the mentioned

Answer: b

Explanation: RIP gives a full route table update every 30 seconds.

7. ENHANCED INTERIOR GATEWAY ROUTING PROTOCOL (EIGRP)

1. What is EIGRP?

Enhanced interior gateway routing protocol (EIGRP) is an advanced distance-vector routing protocol that is used on a computer network for automating routing decisions and configuration. The protocol was designed by cisco systems as a proprietary protocol, available only on cisco routers.

2. What are the different tables in EIGRP?

Neighbor table: the neighbor relationships are tracked in this table which are the basis for EIGRP routing and convergence activity. The address and the interface of a neighbor is discovered and recorded in a new entry of the neighbor table, whenever a new neighbor is discovered. These tables are used for reliable and sequenced delivery of packets.

Topology table: routers use topology table which route traffic in a network. All routing tables inside the autonomous system are available in this table, where the router is positioned. Each router uses routing protocol and maintains a topology table for each configured network protocol. The routes leading to a destination are found in the topology table.

Route table: the routes of particular destinations are stored in the routing tables. The information contains the network topology that is immediately around it. The primary goal of routing protocols and routes is the construction of routing tables. Network id, cost of the packet path and next hop are the details are available in the routing table.

3. Why EIGRP is called hybrid protocol?

EIGRP can be referred to as a hybrid protocol. It combines most of the characteristics of traditional distance vector protocols with some characteristics of link-state protocols.

4. Explain the different types of packets in EIGRP.
- **Hello packets:** EIGRP neighbor ship is discovered and maintained by hello packets. If the router fails to receive a hello packet within the hold timer, the corresponding router will be declared dead.
- **Update packets:** at the time of discovering new neighbor, update packets are sent, so that the topology table can be built by the neighbor router. Update packets are unicast and always transmitted reliably.
- Query packets: when the destination goes into active state, the query packets are sent. Query packets are multicast and replies are always sent in reply to the queries for indicating the originator that it does not need to go into active state.
- **Reply packets:** when the destination goes into active state, the reply packets are sent. Reply packets are unicast to the originator of the query and transmission of reply packets are reliable.

- Ack packets: ack packets use to know the transmission status. If a hello packet sent without data is also recognized as acknowledgement. Unicast address with non-zero acknowledgement number is always sent by acks.

5.   **What is meant by active and passive states in EIGRP?**

An EIGRP route can exist in one of two states, in the topology table:

- Active State
- Passive State

A passive state indicates that a route is reachable, and that EIGRP is fully converged. A stable EIGRP network will have all routes in a passive state. Routes are placed in an active state when the successor and any feasible Successors fail, forcing the EIGRP to send out query packets and re-converge. Multiple routes in an active state indicate an unstable EIGRP Network. If a feasible successor exists, a route should never enter an active State. Routes will become stuck-in-active (sia) when a router sends out a query Packet but does not receive a reply packet within three minutes. In other Words, a route will become sia if EIGRP fails to re-converge. The local Router will clear the neighbor adjacency with any router(s) that has failed to reply and will place all routes from that neighbor(s) in an active state.

6.   **What is the different k-values used in EIGRP?**

EIGRP uses different k values to determine the best path to each destination.

- Bandwidth (k1) Load (k2)
- Delay (k3)
- Reliability (k4) MTU (k5)

7.   **Conditions for EIGRP neighbors.**
Both routers must be in the same primary subnet both routers must be configured to use the same k-values both routers must in the same as both routers must have the same authentication configuration (within reason) the interfaces facing each other must not be passive.

8.   **Should i always use the EIGRP log-neighbor-changes command when i configure EIGRP?**

Yes, this command makes it easy to determine why an EIGRP neighbor was reset. This reduces troubleshooting time.

9.   **Does EIGRP support secondary addresses?**

EIGRP does support secondary addresses. Since EIGRP always sources data packets from the primary address, cisco recommends that you configure all routers on a particular subnet with primary addresses that belong to the same subnet. Routers do not form EIGRP neighbors over secondary networks. Therefore, if all of the primary IP addresses of routers do not agree, problems can arise with neighbor adjacencies.

10.   **What is advertised distance?**

Advertised distance or reported distance: The advertised distance (ad) is the distance from a given neighbor to the destination router. Feasible distance: The feasible distance (fd) is the distance from the current router to the destination.

11. **What is the multicast address used by EIGRP to send hello packets?**

224.0.0.10

12. **What types of authentication is supported by EIGRP?**

EIGRP route authentication provides md5 authentication of routing updates from the EIGRP routing protocol. The md5 keyed digest in each EIGRP packet prevents the introduction of unauthorized or false routing messages from unapproved sources.

13. **What is the use of "variance" command in EIGRP?**

EIGRP provides a mechanism to load balance over unequal cost paths through variance command. Variance is a number (1 to 128), multiplied by the local best metric then includes the routes with the lesser or equal metric. The default variance value is 1, which means equal-cost load balancing.

14. **What happen when we enable passive interface in EIGRP?**

With EIGRP running on a network, the passive-interface command stops both outgoing and incoming routing updates, since the effect of the command causes the router to stop sending and receiving hello packets over an interface.

15. **Can i configure more than one EIGRP autonomous system on the same router?**

Yes, you can configure more than one EIGRP autonomous system on the same router. This is typically done at a redistribution point where two EIGRP autonomous systems are interconnected. Individual router interfaces should only be included within a single EIGRP autonomous system.

16. **What Is an Offset-list, And How Is It Useful?**

The offset-list is a feature used to modify the composite metrics in EIGRP. The value configured in the offset-list command is added to the delay value calculated by the router for the route matched by an access-list. An offset-list is the preferred method to influence a particular path that is advertised and/or chosen.

17. **How Can I Tag External Routes in EIGRP?**

You can tag routes that EIGRP has learned from another routing protocol using a 32 bit tag value. Starting with ddts CSCdw22585, internal routes can also be tagged. However, the tag value cannot exceed 255 due to packet limitations for internal routes.

18. **What are different route types in EIGRP?**
1) Internal route—routes that are originated within the autonomous system (as).
2) Summary route—routes that are summarized in the router (for example, internal paths that have been summarized).
3) External route—routes that are redistributed to EIGRP.

19. **What are the various load-balancing options available in EIGRP?**

The offset-list can be used to modify the metrics of routes that EIGRP learns through a particular interface, or pbr can be used.

20.   **What are the primary functions of the PDM?**

EIGRP supports 3 protocol suites: IP, ipv6, and IPX. Each of them has its own PDM. These are the primary functions of PDM:

Maintaining the neighbor and topology tables of EIGRP routers that belong to that protocol suite Building and translating protocol specific packets for dual Interfacing dual to the protocol specific routing table computing the metric and passing this information to dual; dual handles only the picking of the feasible successors (fss) Implement filtering and access lists.

8. OSPF

1. **Explain in your own words OSPF Protocol.**

The OSPF (Open Shortest Path First) protocol is one of a family of IP Routing protocols and is an Interior Gateway Protocol (IGP) for the Internet, used to distribute IP routing information throughout a single Autonomous System (AS) in an IP network.

The OSPF protocol is a link-state routing protocol, which means that the routers exchange topology information with their nearest neighbors. The topology information is flooded throughout the AS, so that every router within the AS has a complete picture of the topology of the AS. This picture is then used to calculate end-to-end paths through the AS, normally using a variant of the Dijkstra algorithm. Therefore, in a link-state routing protocol, the next hop address to which data is forwarded is determined by choosing the best end-to-end path to the eventual destination.

The main advantage of a link state routing protocol like OSPF is that the complete knowledge of topology allows routers to calculate routes that satisfy particular criteria. This can be useful for traffic engineering purposes, where routes can be constrained to meet particular quality of service requirements. The main disadvantage of a link state routing protocol is that it does not scale well as more routers are added to the routing domain. Increasing the number of routers increases the size and frequency of the topology updates, and also the length of time it takes to calculate end-to-end routes. This lack of scalability means that a link state routing protocol is unsuitable for routing across the Internet at large, which is the reason why IGPs only route traffic within a single AS.

Each OSPF router distributes information about its local state (usable interfaces and reachable neighbors, and the cost of using each interface) to other routers using a Link State Advertisement (LSA) message. Each router uses the received messages to build up an identical database that describes the topology of the AS. 1.

2. **What are the advantages of OSPF?**
The advantages of OSPF are:

1) OSPF is not a cisco proprietary protocol.
2) OSPF always determine the loop free routes.
3) If any changes occur in the network, it updates fast.
4) OSPF minimizes the routes and reduces the size of routing table by configuring area.
5) Low bandwidth utilization.
6) Transfers and tags external routes injected into as.
7) Multiple routes are supported.
8) Support variable length subnet masking.
9) It is suitable for large network.

3. **What are the Dis-advantages of OSPF**

The Dis-advantages of OSPF are:

1) OSPF is quite CPU and memory intensive due to SPF algorithm and maintenance of multiple copies of routing information;

2) more complex protocol to implement compared to RIP

4. What are IGP?

An IGP (Interior Gateway Protocol) is a protocol for exchanging routing information between gateways (hosts with routers) within an autonomous network (Companies, organizations, and even service providers use an IGP on their internal networks). IGPs include RIP, EIGRP, OSPF, and IS-IS

5. Describe OSPF Protocol in your own words.

OSPF (Open Shortest Path First) is a router protocol used to find the best path for packets as they pass through a set of connected networks.

- Concept of area, link state routing protocol, all traffic passes through area 0
- Its nature is area is distance vector while passing from area to area
- It has LSAs.
- AD is 110
- metric is dependent on bandwidth
- Algorithm is called Dijkstra's (SPF)
- Maximum routers possible 50.

6. What is the purpose of having OSPF areas?

- efficiency; less SPF calculations so that you can save the processing cycles of the routers

7. Types of OSPF Link Statement Advertisement - LSA, the purpose of each LSA type?

Known LSA types are 7, actually there are 10 as descript in the following table.

LSA	Name	Description
Type 1	Router LSA	Generated by all routers in an area to describe their directly attached links (intra-area routes). Does not leave the area
Type 2	Network LSA	Generated by the DR of a broadcast or non-broadcast segment to describe the neighbors connected to That segment. Does not leave the area
Type 3	Summary LSA	Generated by the area border router (ABR) to describe a route to neighbors outside the area (inter-area route).
Type 4	Summary LSA	Generated by the ABR to describe a route to an autonomous system border router (ASBR) to neighbors outside the area.
Type 5	External L SA	Generated by the ASBR to describe routes redistributed into the area These routes appear as El or E2 in the IP routing table. E2 (default) uses a static cost throughout the OSPF domain, as it only takes the cost into account that is reported at redistribution. El uses a cumulative cost of the cost reported into the OSPF domain at

57

		redistribution plus the local cost to the ASBR
Type 6	Multicast LSA	Used in multicast OSPF. Not supported by Cisco.
Type 7	NSSA External LSA	Generated by an ASBR inside a not-so-stubby (NSSA) area to describe routes redistributed into the NSSA area LSA 7 is translated into LSA 5 as it leaves the NSSA area These routes appear as Ni or N2 in the IP routing table inside the NSSA area Much like LSA 5, N2 is a static cost while N1 is a cumulative cost that includes the cost up to the ASBR.
Type9/10/11	Opaque-LSA	OSFP extensions, graceful LSA used to support GR is type 9 LSA example, type 10 LSA is used to support TE

Table 6 Purpose of each LSA type

8. What exact LSA type you can see in different areas

- In normal area you can see 1,2,3,5
- in NSSA you can only see 7
- in stub area you can only see 7

Area vise LSA Types mention in the following table.

Area	Restriction
Normal	None
Stub	No Type 5 AS-external LSA allowed
Totally Stub	No Type 3, 4 or 5 LSAs allowed except the default summary route
NSSA	No Type 5 AS-external LSAs allowed, but Type 7 LSAs that convert to Type 5 at the NSSA ABR can traverse
NSSA Totally Stub	No Type 3, 4 or 5 LSAs except the default summary route, but Type 7 LSAs that convert to Type 5 at the NSSA ABR are allowed

Table 7 LSA type in different areas vise

This table 1 shows the differences between the types of areas defined in this document:

OSPF LSAs and OSPF Area Type							
Area Type	LSA 1	LSA 2	LSA 3	LSA 4	LSA 5	LSA 6	LSA 7
Backbone Area	Yes	Yes	Yes	Yes	Yes	Yes	No
Non-Backbone Area	Yes	Yes	Yes	Yes	Yes	Yes	No
Stub	Yes	Yes	Yes	Yes	No	No	No
Totally stubby	Yes	Yes	No	No	No	No	No
Not-so-stubby	Yes	Yes	Yes	Yes	Yes	No	Yes

Table 8 OSPF LSAs and OSPF Area Type

9. **How OSPF establishes neighbor relation, what are the stages?**

OSPF Adjacency States
- Down
- ATTEMPT
- INIT
- 2-WAY   ------------------ > except DR/BDR all the routers remain on this stage.
- EXSTART
- EXCHANGE
- LOADING
- FULL

10. **If OSPF router is stuck in each stage what the problem is and how to troubleshoot it?**

Reason for Neighbor Adjacency Problem	Commands for Diagnosing the Problem
OSPF is not configured on one of the routers.	show ip ospf
OSPF is not enabled on an interface where it is needed.	show ip ospf interface
OSPF HELLO or Dead timer interval values are mismatched.	show ip ospf interface
ip ospf network-type mismatch on the adjoining interfaces.	show ip ospf interface
MTU mismatch between neighboring interfaces.	show interface <int-type><int-num>
OSPF area-type is stub on one neighbor, but the adjoining neighbor in the same area is not configured for stub.	show running-config show ip ospf interface
OSPF neighbors have duplicate Router IDs.	show ip ospf show ip ospf interface
OSPF is configured on the secondary network of the neighbor, but not on the primary network. This is an illegal configuration which prevents OSPF from being enabled on the interface.	show ip ospf interface show running-config
OSPF HELLOs are not processed due to a lack of resources, such as high CPU utilization or not enough memory.	show memory summary show memory processor
An underlying Layer problem prevents OSPF HELLOs from being received.	show interface

Table 9 In OSPF Reason for Neighbor Adjacency Problem

11. **Can you discuss in brief how does the OSPF hierarchy looks like in a single area or in a multi areas. ?**

- 2 level hierarchy
- OSPF area 0 is a parent, rest of the areas are child

12. **What is the behavior of OSPF in broadcast and non-broadcast networks ?**

BROADCAST – CISCO EXTENSION:

- Has one IP subnet
- Uses Multicast OSPF Hello packets to discover neighbors
- Elects DR And BDR
- Requires a Full-Mesh or Partial-Mesh topology

NONBROADCAST (NBMA) – RFC 2328:

- Has one IP subnet
- Requires neighbors to be manually configured
- Elects DR and BDR
- requires that the DR and BDR have full connectivity with all other routers
- typically used in a full-mesh or partial-mesh topology

13. **Draw the diagram of typical OSPF network and explain generally how it works, DR, BDR, election, ASBR, ABR, route redistribution and summarization.**

    Draw the Diagram of a Typical OSPF Network and Explain Generally How It Works: DR, BDR, Election, ASBR, ABR, Route Redistribution, and Summarization.2.

    This question is a great one and often makes the interviewee wonder where to start. Intentionally open ended, the responses vary widely. What you should convey in your answer is an in-depth knowledge of OSPF. Scratch the surface and dive in deeper if you see positive responses from your interviewers.

    Preferably using a whiteboard, start with the hierarchy of OSPF — a two-level model — and draw a diagram like the one as shown below.

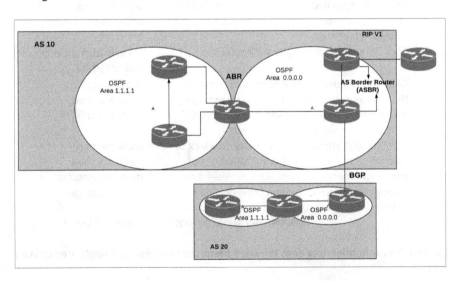

Figure 16 Diagram of a Typical OSPF Network & How It Works

Discuss having a backbone Area 0 (or 0.0.0.0) and that all areas must connect to the backbone area. Other area types include the following: stub area (an area that does not receive AS external routes); total stubby area (an area that does not allow summary routes or external routes); and not-so-stubby area (an area that can import AS external routes and send them to the backbone area, but will not receive AS external routes from the backbone or other areas). You want to include the type of routers contained in the hierarchy: internal routers, area border routers (ABR), backbone routers, and autonomous system boundary routers (ASBR). Mention that the shortest path first (SPF) calculation is performed independently on each area. You should state that the time to converge is faster than distance-vector routing protocols (DVRPs) such as RIP. Include a brief statement on the low bandwidth requirement for LSAs. Also mention support for classless routing, Variable-Length Subnet Masking (VLSM), authentication, and multipath statements.

Describe the OSPF algorithm and generally how it works: Changes in the network generate LSAs, routers exchange the LSAs, and each router builds and maintains its own database. So, if the network is in a steady state, there will be refresh LSAs only every 30 minutes. You want to cover the five types of routing protocol packets: Hello, Database description, Link-state request, Link-state update, and Link-state

acknowledgment. Hello packets are multicast on 224.0.0.5 and routers use them to form adjacency relationships.

You want to cover the types of Link State Advertisements (LSAs): Router link (LSA type 1), Network link (LSA type 2), Network summary (LSA type 3), ASBR (LSA type 4), External (LSA type 5), and NSSA external (LSA type 7). Do not neglect a discussion on IPv6 and that OSPFv3 supports it. You might want to discuss briefly how vendors implement OSPFv3 using a ships-in-the-night approach to support both v3 and v2 simultaneously. OSPFv3 distributes IPv6 prefixes and uses the same interfaces

and nearly the same LSA types as OSPFv2. It uses the same methods for neighbor discovery and adjacency forming. The only differences are that OSPFv3 has to use a network link rather than a subnet.

And there can be multiple instances of OSPFv3 on a given link. You should mention that the topology in OSPFv3 is a bit different as well — using a router ID and Link ID. And because OSPFv3 uses links, there's a new Link LSA type as well as an Intra-Area Prefix LSA for the IPv6 prefixes.

To fully answer the question, you have to go through the process of neighbor finding and adjacency creation. Routers sharing a common network segment or link will become neighbors using the Hello protocol. Routers send Hello packets out each interface with the multicast address of 224.0.0.5. When a router sees its own primary address in a Hello packet from another router, the routers are then neighbors. As

neighbors, the routers have to agree on the following things: the area-id (of the area they belong to); a preshared password (for authentication); hello and dead intervals (how often hello packets are sent and how long to wait to for a neighbor's hello); and a stub area flag (whether the router is in a stub area). Neighbor routers then form adjacencies. When the routers exchange their databases, they are adjacent. To limit the volume of information exchanged on a network segment, routers go through an election process. This election nominates a designated router (DR) and a backup designated router (BDR). The DR is the sole source for updates on the segment. All other routers on the segment exchange route information with the DR and BDR. Area Border Routers (ABRs) collect all the routes for the area and combine/

summarize them into a single advertisement to the backbone area (inter-area route summarization). The backbone routers then forward these summarized routes. External route summarization may occur as well when distributing the routes to another protocol.

14. Difference between RIPv1 and RIPv2?

RIPv1	RIPv2
Classful	Classless
Automatic summarization to the class boundary	Manual summarization on per interface basis
Network masks not included in the advertisements	Network masks included in the advertisements
Advertisements use broadcast destination address 255.255.255.255	Advertisements use reserved multicast destination address 224.0.0.9
No authentication support	2 authentication methods {clear text, MD5)

Table 10 Difference between RIPv1 and RIPv2

15. How many numbers of routes carried by RIP packet?

25 routes are carried by a rip packet
In OSPF - It's LSA so it is open

16. Is OSPF link state or distance vector or path vector protocol?

Link State Protocol

17. What's the difference between Distance Vector and Link State Routing Protocols?

Dynamic routing protocols are categorized as either distance-vector protocols or link-state protocols

Distance-Vector Routing Protocols
- The full routing table is sent in periodic updates to neighbors, which requires more bandwidth
- Distance is the main metric used to calculate routes
  - RIP uses hop count
  - IGRP uses bandwidth and delay
- Slower to converge because it has to wait for the periodic updates
- More susceptible to loops
- Distance-Vector Protocols - RIP, IGRP
- Routers rely on neighbors for route information - routing by rumor

Link-State Routing Protocols
- Created to avoid the convergence and loop issues of Distance-Vector protocols
- Routers send updates that advertise the state of their links. The full routing table is not sent, which saves on bandwidth.
- Cost is the metric used to calculate routes

- Areas are used to define which routers share updates with each other
- Routers know the state of all links within their area
- Routers use different tables to maintain an understanding of the Link-States
  - Neighbor table - list of neighbor routers and the interface
  - Topology table - the Link-State table, map of all links within an area and their status
  - Shortest-Path table - best routes to each particular destination - this is the routing table
- Convergence is quick
- Loops are avoided
- Because of the three tables needing to be maintained, it could use more RAM and CPU resources.

18. What is the difference between OSPF and IS-IS and which one is preferred?

- IS-IS is based on MAC
- OSPF is based on L3 - IP
- OSPF supports NBMA and point-to-multipoint links, IS-IS does not.
- IS-IS rides directly above layer two, versus on IP like OSPF, which may offer a security advantage (IS-IS attacks cannot be routed).
- OSPF can support virtual links, IS-IS cannot (because it rides L2 directly).
- On broadcast networks, OSPF elects a DR and BDR which cannot be preempted, whereas IS-IS elects only a single DIS which may be preempted.
- OSPF designates a backbone area (area 0) for inter-area advertisements; IS-IS organizes the domain into two layers.
- OSPF routers can belong to multiple areas, IS-IS routers belong to exactly one area.
- OSPF has more strict requirements for forming neighbor adjacencies. The hello and dead intervals must match, and the subnet mask must match (except on point-to-point links)

19. How many network types available in OSPF?

According to RFC 2328 section 1.2, there are three major network types defined in OSPF:

1) Point-to-point networks
2) Broadcast networks
3) Non-broadcast networks which is sub-divided into non-broadcast multi-access (NBMA) networks and point-to-multipoint networks.

For more detail information.3.

Network Type	DR/BDR?	Default Hello Interval	Dynamic Neighbor Discovery?	Default for...
Broadcast	yes	10	yes	Ethernet
P2P	no	10	yes	FR P2P
NBMA	yes	30	no	FR physical and multipoint
point-to-multipoint (NBMA)	no	30	no	
point-to-multipoint	no	30	yes	/32 subnets only
loopback	no	---	---	/32 subnets only

Table 11 Network types available in OSPF

As you can see, each network type has a different response to DR/BDR formation, different hello interval, dynamic neighbor discovery, and most are set as the default for a different type of network. (Also, for purposes of the R&S NP, these differences are very important. I memorized this table for interview.)

20. **LSA 3 and LSA 4 are generated by which router?**

LSA 4: ASBR information
These are generated by ABR; Injected by an ABR into the backbone to advertise the presence of an ASBR within an area.

LSA 3: Inter area route
Generated by an ABR and advertised among areas

21. **When to use Stub and Not So Stubby Area?**
   - Stub is used when no distribution is taking place
   - NSSA when distribution is happening

22. **How to get the external routes without making area Not So Stubby?**
   Tunnel is the solution

23. **What is the different type of route summarization available in OSPF?**
   OSPF allows for two forms of summarization.
   1) One form of summarization is used when summarizing routes redistributed in to OSPF from another routing protocol.
   2) The other form of summarization is used when summarizing an area. With both forms of summarization, summary LSAs are created and flooded toward Location 0, or the central source area. The backbone location, in turn, floods the URL states to the other areas.

24. **If any of the OSPF area is not stabilized, does it impact another area?**

If the area 0 is not stable then the SPF will be calculated with in the area0 for LSA1 and LSA 2 these LSAs are summary LSAs for the other areas, so other area routers will calculate the SPF for summary LSA, whenever wrong happens in area 0.

25. What is the use of forwarding address in LSA 5 and LSA 7 in OSPF?

In scenarios where we have multiple ABRs converting/translating same network from Type7 to Type5 LSA, then OSPF database need to act on only one of them. The other must withdraw its LSA. This is one of many loop avoidance techniques adopted in OSPF.

The RFC 2328 says "if two routers, both reachable from one another, originate functionally equivalent AS-external-LSAs (i.e., same destination, cost and non-zero forwarding address), then the LSA originated by the router having the highest OSPF Router ID is used. The router having the lower OSPF Router ID can then flush its LSA.

The forwarding address is an important concept in the Type 7 LSA and when it gets converted to Type 5 LSA by NSSA-ABR. [1]

26. If loopback is not configured, what will be the router-id selected by OSPF process?

A RID is the highest logical (loopback) IP address configured on a router, if no logical/loopback IP address is set then the Router uses the highest IP address configured on its active interfaces.

27. Can we run multiple OSPF process in single router and what is the advantage of such a network design?

Yes, it is possible. if a router is running 2 separate OSPF processes then each process can have its own separate area 0.

The implications of running separate OSPF processes include these:

- an interface can be active in only 1 interface. So, each OSPF process will have a unique set of neighbors.
- each OSPF process will learn its own prefixes and maintain those prefixes in its own database.
- each OSPF process will advertise only prefixes from its own data base. The only way to have one process advertise prefixes from the other process is to redistribute.

And the separate OSPF processes have separate OSPF data bases and the separate OSPF processes do not share any data with the other OSPF process unless you redistribute.

No there are not separate RIBs. There is a single routing table for the router which will contain routes from both OSPF processes. But each OSPF process will advertise only the routes that are contained in its own database.

If you run 2 OSPF processes and if each process learns the same prefix then each OSPF process will attempt to insert its route into the routing table. If both prefixes have the same metric them both routes will show up in the routing table (and the router will load share traffic to that destination). Note that since both processes cannot run on the same interface, the 2 routes that it learns will have different next hop addresses - it is not possible for both OSPF processes to learn the same prefix with the same next hop. [2]

28. **What are timers of OSPF?**

Hello and Dead Timer

29. **Multicast address of used by OSPF.**

Allspf address 224.0.0.5 Rest of the router does it
Allspf address 224.0.0.6 (DR/BDR multicasts on this address)

30. **OSPF works on which layer? Reason**

Layer 3

31. **What is backbone area in OSPF?**

The backbone area (Area 0) is the core of an OSPF network. All other areas are connected to it and all traffic between areas must traverse it. All routing between areas is distributed through the backbone area.

32. **Can we use OSPF without backbone area? Reason?**

No.

33. **Is it required that OSPF router-id must be reachable in IGP cloud?**

It is required. - Example is OPSF TShoot in MSDP, especially necessary for moving from one area to another

34. **OSPF neighborship is not coming up. Please tell the various steps to troubleshoot it.**

- Check OSPF hello ad dead timer should be same
- network mask of both interfaces should be same
- MTU size should be same - or MTU ignore must be
- Area ID should be the same
- Authentication be checked

35. **One side MTU is 1500 and another side MTU is 1600. Does it affect neighborship? How to fix**

Yes, it does
- either ip ospf mtu-ignore, or change it to 1500
- or change the mtu to 1500 on the other end

36. **Provide process of DR and BDR election.**

Within OSPF, the role of the Designated Router (DR) and a Backup Designated Router (BDR) is to act as a central point for exchanging of OSPF information between multiple routers on the same, multi-access broadcast network segment.

Upon the segment each router will go through an election process, to elect a DR and BDR. There are two rules used to determine who is elected:

1. **Priority** - Router with the highest wins the election. The default priority is 1. This is configured on a per-interface level.

2. **Router ID** - If there is a tie, the highest router ID wins the election.

37. **If DR is down and no BDR is configured what will happen?**

Based on the network type, OSPF router can elect one router to be a Designated Router (DR) and one router to be a Backup Designated Router (BDR). For example, on multiaccess broadcast networks (such as LANs) routers defaults to elect a DR and BDR. DR and BDR serve as the central point for exchanging OSPF routing information. Each non-DR or non-BDR router will exchange routing information only with the DR and BDR, instead of exchanging updates with every router on the network segment. DR will then distribute topology information to every other router inside the same area, which greatly reduces OSPF traffic.

To send routing information to a DR or BDR the multicast address of 224.0.0.6 is used. DR sends routing updates to the multicast address of 224.0.0.5. If DR fails, BDR takes over its role of redistributing routing information.

Every router on a network segment will establish a full neighbor relationship with the DR and BDR. Non-DR and non-BDR routers will establish a two-way neighbor relationship between themselves.

NOTE

On point-to-point links, a DR and BDR are not elected since only two routers are directly connected.

On LANs, DR and BDR have to be elected. Two rules are used to elect a DR and BDR:

1) router with the highest OSPF priority will become a DR. By default, all routers have a priority of 1.
2) if there is a tie, a router with the highest router ID wins the election.

38. What is the difference between a neighbor and adjacency?

Two OSPF routers are neighbors if they are connected to the same subnet and share a series of common configuration information. In particular, two OSPF neighbors do not exchange any routing information. OSPF adjacency is formed between selected neighbors and allows them to exchange routing information. So, two routers must first be neighbors, only then they can become adjacent.

So, two routers must first be neighbors, only then they can become adjacent. Two routers become adjacent if:

- At least one of them is DR or BDR (on multi-access type networks), or

- They are interconnected by a point-to-point or point-to-multipoint network type. [3]

39. My OSPF neighborship is showing 2-way, what does it mean?
It's not a DR/BDR and the neighbors is good

40. OSPF external routes are not redistributing, how to make it happen?
LSA conversion is not happening.

41. Which of the following is not a characteristic of link-state routing protocols?
A. They respond quickly to network changes.
B. They broadcast every 30 minutes.

C. They send triggered updates when a network change occurs.
D. They may send periodic updates, known as link-state refresh, at long time intervals, such as every 30 minutes.

Answer?

42. For all the routers in the network to make consistent routing decisions, each link-state router must keep a record of all the following items except which one?

A. Its immediate neighbor routers
B. All of the other routers in the network, or in its area of the network, and their attached Networks
C. The best paths to each destination
D. The version of the routing protocol used

Answer D

43. Which of the following is not a characteristic of an OSPF area?
    A. It may minimize routing table entries.
    B. It requires a flat network design.
    C. It may localize the impact of a topology change within an area.
    D. It may stop detailed LSA flooding at the area boundary.

44. True or false: An ABR connects area 0 to the no backbone areas.

Answer? Yes

An area is a set of routers that are administratively configured to exchange link-state information with each other. There is one special area—the backbone area, also known as area 0. An example of a routing domain divided into areas as shown in the figure, Routers R1, R2, and R3 are members of the backbone area. They are also members of at least one non-backbone area; R1 is actually a member of both area 1 and area 2. A router that is a member of both the backbone area and a non-backbone area is an area border router (ABR). Note that these are distinct from the routers that are at the edge of an AS, which are referred to as AS border routers for clarity.

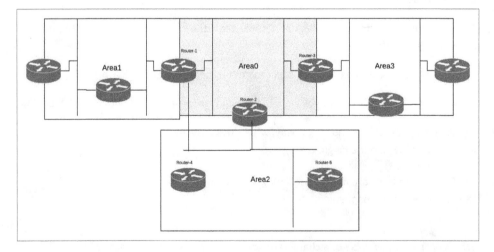

Figure 17 Area1, Area2 and Area3 connected with Area0

45. **When a router receives an LSA (within an LSU), it does not do which of the following?**

    a) If the LSA entry does not already exist, the router adds the entry to its LSDB, sends back an LSAck, floods the information to other routers, runs SPF, and updates its routing table.

    b) If the entry already exists and the received LSA has the same sequence number, the router overwrites the information in the LSDB with the new LSA entry.

    c) If the entry already exists but the LSA includes newer information (it has a higher sequence number), the router adds the entry to its LSDB, sends back an LSAck, floods the information to other routers, runs SPF, and updates its routing table.

    d) If the entry already exists but the LSA includes older information, it sends an LSU to the sender with its newer information.

46. **What is an OSPF type 2 packet?**

    A. Database description (DBD), which checks for database synchronization between routers
    B. Link-state request (LSR), which requests specific link-state records from router to router
    C. Link-state update (LSU), which sends specifically, requested link-state records
    D. Link-state acknowledgment (LSAck), which acknowledges the other packet types

Answer A
Network (Type 2) LSAs to build their topology tables. Once fully synchronized, routers within an area will all have identical topology tables.

47. **Which of the following is true of hellos and dead intervals?**
    A. They don't need to be the same on neighboring routers, because the lowest common denominator is adopted.
    B. They don't need to be the same on neighboring routers, because the highest common denominator is adopted.
    C. They don't need to be the same on neighboring routers, because it is a negotiated interval between neighboring routers.
    D. They need to be the same on neighboring routers.

Answer C

48. **Which IP address is used to send an updated LSA entry to OSPF DRs and BDRs?**
    A. Unicast 224.0.0.5
    B. Unicast 224.0.0.6
    C. Multicast 224.0.0.5
    D. Multicast 224.0.0.6

Answer C
OSPF traffic is multicast either to address 224.0.0.5 (all OSPF routers) or 224.0.0.6 (all Designated   Routers).

49. **To ensure an accurate database; how often does OSPF flood (refresh) each LSA record?**
    A. Every 60 minutes.
    B. Every 30 minutes.
    C. Every 60 seconds.
    D. Every 30 seconds.

E. Flooding each LSA record would defeat the purpose of a link-state routing protocol, that strives to reduce the amount of routing traffic it generates.

Answer B

OSPF sends updates (LSAs) when there is a change to one of its links and will only send the change in the update. LSAs are additionally refreshed every 30 minutes.

50. **What command is used to display the router ID, timers, and statistics?**
    A. Show ip ospf
    B. Show ip ospf neighbors
    C. Show ip ospf stats
    D. Show ip ospf neighborship

Answer A

The show ip ospf command provides the following information:
- The local Router ID.
- SPF Scheduling information, and various SPF timers.
- The number of interfaces in specific areas, including the type of area.
- The link-state age timer.
- The sequence number and checksum for each entry.

51. **Which of the following is not a way in which the OSPF router ID (a unique IP address) can be assigned?**
    A. The highest IP address of any physical interface
    B. The lowest IP address of any physical interface
    C. The IP address of a loopback interface
    D. The router-id command

Answer B

Each OSPF router is identified by a unique Router ID. The Router ID can be determined in one of three ways:
- The Router ID can be manually specified.
- If not manually specified, the highest IP address configured on any Loopback interface on the router will become the Router ID.
- If no loopback interface exists, the highest IP address configured on
- any Physical interface will become the Router ID.

52. **True or false: On point-to-point networks, the router dynamically detects its neighboring routers by multicasting its hello packets to all SPF routers using the address 224.0.0.6.**

Answer True

The IPv4 multicast addresses used for OSPF are 224.0.0.5 to send information to all OSPF routers and 224.0.0.6 to send information to DR/BDR routers

53. **An adjacency is the relationship that exists where?**
    A. Between routers located on the same physical network
    B. Between routers in different OSPF areas
    C. Between a router and its DR and BDR on different networks
    D. Between a backbone DR and a transit BDR

Answer A

OSPF will form neighbor relationships with adjacent routers in the same Area

54. **Which of the following is not true of OSPF point-to-multipoint mode?**
    A. It does not require a full-mesh network.
    B. It does not require a static neighbor configuration.
    C. It uses multiple IP subnets.

D. It duplicates LSA packets.

Answer B

In point to multipoint, Neighbors do not need to be manually specified, so it should be static.

55. **What is the default OSPF mode on a point-to-point Frame Relay sub-interface?**

A. Point-to-point mode
B. Multipoint mode
C. Non broadcast mode
D. Broadcast mode

Answer D

Point-to-point sub interface can only possibly have two devices on it, and from an interface perspective, broadcasts are supported. OSPF treats it as a point-to-point network type

56. **What is the default OSPF mode on a Frame Relay multipoint sub-interface?**

A. Point-to-point mode
B. Multipoint mode
C. Nonbroadcast mode
D. Broadcast mode

Answer C

Point-to-Multipoint sub interfaces really function just like a physical interface does in terms of there being the potential for multiple devices connected to the "interface". OSPF treats this as a non-broadcast network type.

57. **What is the default OSPF mode on a main Frame Relay interface?**

A. Point-to-point mode
B. Multipoint mode
C. Nonbroadcast mode
D. Broadcast mode

Answer C

Frame Relay physical interface is a multipoint interface by nature. OSPF treats it as a non-broadcast network type.

58. Which command displays the number of times that the OSPF Shortest Path First (SPF)

algorithm has been executed?

A. show ip protocol
B. show ip ospf interface
C. show ip ospf
D. show ip ospf database

Answer C

59. What are the OSPF troubleshooting commands?

Commands	Purpose
Router# show ip ospf virtual-links	To display information about OSPF virtual-links:
Router# show ip ospf border-routers	To display routes to both ABRs and ASBRs:
Router# debug ip ospf adj Router# debug ip ospf events Router# debug ip ospf hello	To debug OSPF in real-time
Router# show ip ospf neighbor	To view the OSPF Neighbor Table
Router# show ip ospf database	Router# show ip ospf database

Table 12 OSPF command

9. BGP

1. Explain in your own words BGP Protocol

BGP is a standardized exterior gateway protocol (EGP), as opposed to RIP, OSPF, and EIGRP which are interior gateway protocols (IGP's). BGP Version 4 (BGPv4) is the current standard deployment.

BGP is considered a "Path Vector" routing protocol. BGP was not built to route within an Autonomous System (AS), but rather to route between AS's.

BGP maintains a separate routing table based on shortest AS Path and various other attributes, as opposed to IGP metrics like distance or cost. BGP is the routing protocol of choice on the Internet. Essentially, the Internet is a collection of interconnected Autonomous Systems. BGP Autonomous Systems are assigned an Autonomous System Number (ASN), which is a 16-bit number ranging from 1 – 65535. A specific subset of this range, 64512 – 65535, has been reserved for private (or internal) use.

BGP utilizes TCP for reliable transfer of its packets, on port 179.

2. Is BGP a IGP or EGP?

The Border Gateway Protocol (BGP) is the only currently viable EGP and is the official routing protocol used by the Internet.

3. Differentiate between eBGP and iBGP?

BGP: internal BGP runs between routers in the same AS.

EBGP: routes received from an EBGP peer can be advertised to EBGP and IBGP peers.

The main difference between the two is EBGP runs between two BGP routers in different Autonomous System (AS), however, IBGP runs between two BGP routers in the same AS.

4. BGP is link state or distance vector protocol?

BGP is the path-vector protocol that provides routing information for autonomous systems on the Internet via its AS-Path attribute.

5. Which TCP port is used by BGP for communication?

BGP uses TCP port 179 to communicate with other routers. A BGP speaker sends 19-byte keep-alive messages every 60 seconds to maintain the connection. Among routing protocols, BGP is unique in using TCP as its transport protocol.

6. When should you use BGP?

BGP is not a necessity when multiple connections to the Internet are required. Fault tolerance or redundancy of outbound traffic can easily be handled by an IGP, such as OSPF or EIGRP.

BGP is also completely unnecessary if there is only one connection to an external AS (such as the Internet). There are over 100,000 routes on the Internet, and interior routers should not be needlessly burdened.

BGP should be used under the following circumstances:
- Multiple connections exist to external AS's (such as the Internet) via different providers.
- Multiple connections exist to external AS's through the same provider but connect via a separate CO or routing policy.
- The existing routing equipment can handle the additional demands.

BGP's true benefit is in controlling how traffic enters the local AS, rather than how traffic exits it.

7. Can I use BGP instead of any IGP?

There are reasons why BGP is **NOT** recommended to replace an IGP, the most evident are:
1) The full-mesh necessary for all iBGP-connected routers if running without any IGP
2) Slow convergence when default timers left.
3) Not available on low-end routers or L3 switches.

8. Can you run two BGP process on single router?
Nope, however using address families it is possible

9. What is Autonomous System?
Routers and switches, under a control of a single authority. Represented by a unique ASN

10. Types of BGP routing table? 3 tables
a. Routing information base
b. adj RIB in,
c. adj RIB out,
d. Loc RIB

11. What is the BGP path selection criterion?

1. **Largest Weight** (locally originated paths: 32768, other 0) - AFFECE TTHE ROUTERS
2. **Largest Local-Preference** ("bgp default local-preference") default 100 - AFFECTS THE AS
3. **Prefer local paths** (decreasing preference: default-originate in neighbor, default-information-originate in global, network, redistribute, aggregate)
4. **Shortest AS_PATH** ("bgp best path as-path ignore" bypasses this step; AS_SET counts as 1; AS_CONFED_SEQUENCE and AS_CONFED_SET are not counted)
5. **Lowest origin code** (0-IGP, 1-EGP, 2-Incomplete)
6. Lowest MED (bgp always-compare-med; bgp bestpath med-confed; bgp bestpath med missing-as-worst; bgp deterministic-med) default 0
7. eBGP preferred over iBGP (Confed. paths are treated as internal paths)
8. Closest IGP neighbor (best cost)
9. Determine if multiple paths require installation (multipath)

10. If paths are external choose the oldest one (flap prevention). Skipped if „bgp bestpath compare-routerid")
11. Lowest Router-ID
12. Minimum Cluster-List length (RR environment)
13. Lowest neighbor address

12. What is the easiest way to remember the BGP Attributes?

To remember BGP Best Path Algorithm, use the following mnemonic as shown in the following table.

"We Love Oranges AS Oranges Mean Pure Refreshment"	
W	Weight (Highest)
L	LOCAL_PREF (Highest)
O	Originate (local)
AS	AS_PATH (shortest)
O	ORIGIN Code (IGP > EGP > Incomplete)
M	MED (lowest)
P	Paths (External > Internal)
R	RID (lowest)

Table 13 Remember method for BGP Best Path Algorithm

13. Define various BGP path attributes.

The BGP attributes help in determining the paths to a remote network.

14. Why weight doesn't fall under path attribute category?
a. It's proprietary
b. It's never included in update packets.
c. It is used within the AS
d.

15. What is confederation?

In network routing, **BGP confederation** is a method to use Border Gateway Protocol (**BGP**) to subdivide a single autonomous system (AS) into multiple internal sub-AS's, yet still advertise as a single AS to external peers. The intent is to reduce iBGP mesh size.

BGP confederations are another way to solve the scaling problems created by the **BGP** full mesh requirement. **BGP confederations** effectively break up a large autonomous system (AS) into sub-autonomous systems (sub-ASs). Each sub-AS must be uniquely identified within the **confederation**-AS by a sub-AS number. AS divides into small AS, they consider the routes as ebgp between the AS.

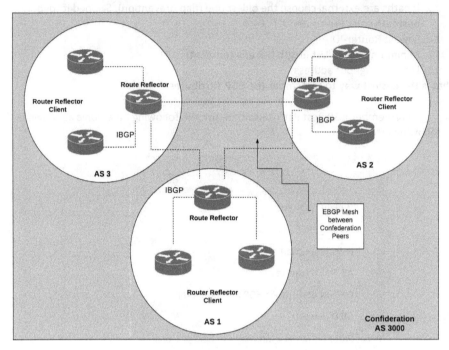

Figure 18 BGP confederation

16. What is route reflector and why it is required?

RR is Just like OSPF DR. IT distributes routes to other Routers. It is required when the neighbors are not fully meshed.

Route reflectors (RR) are one method to get rid of the full-mesh of IBGP peers in your network. The other method is BGP confederations. The **route reflector** allows all IBGP speakers within your autonomous network to learn about the available routes without introducing loops.

Route reflectors distribute iBGP information from one router to another, which is normally not allowed in iBGP. Since the clients of the route reflector get all iBGP from the route reflector they don't need to have iBGP sessions with all other BGP routers. Reflectors add additional path attributes that allow them to detect and eliminate loops.

In a confederation, the AS is split into a number of sub-ASes, so the iBGP full mesh is done within each sub-AS and a modified version of eBGP is used between sub-ASes. To the outside, the confederation behaves like a single AS.

17. What is no-synchronization rule?

- The route needs to be learnt from IGP before being selected as the best path.
- It's a loop prevention mechanism.
- To avoid a blackhole created because some of routers in between don't have the BGP running (a>b>c)

18. What are Default BGP timers?

- Keepalives are sent 60 seconds
- updates are never sent
- periodic updates are 5 & 30 seconds for internal and external peers

19. When does BGP use 0.0.0.0 router id?

If BGP process has started without assigning interface IP address

is this possible on OSPF ?

20. Does route reflector come in actual path during traffic forwarding?

Route does go through the RR but not the actual traffic does pass through the RR.

21. What is Site of Origin aka SOO?

It's an attribute, used in MPLS

BGP extended community < more details in the Routing bits >

22. What is the cost of external and internal BGP routes?

This question is intended to confuse the candidate. BGP is not a typical protocol it is an application that run on TCP port 179. It is different than other routing protocols because for best path selection router read instruction code and take decision on the base of attribute and it counts number of Autonomous System (AS) numbers.

The correct answer to this question is as follows

BGP is dynamic routing protocol, and it is algorithm less protocol. Note if administrator want to manipulate the BJP default route preference than you just change the path attributes value, no need to change bandwidth and other metrics which happened like in EIGRP, OSPF etc. BGP determines the best path by successively comparing the attributes of each "route pair." The attributes are compared in a specific order:

- *Weight – Which route has the highest weight?*
- *Local Preference – Which route has the highest local preference?*
- *Locally Originated – Did the local router originate this route? In other words, is the next hop to the destination 0.0.0.0?*
- *AS-Path – Which route has the shortest AS-Path?*
- *Origin Code – Where did the route originate? The following origin*
- *MED – Which path has the lowest MED?*
- *BGP Route Type – Is this an eBGP or iBGP route? (eBGP routes are*
- *preferred)*
- *Age – Which route is the oldest? (oldest is preferred)*
- *Router ID – Which route originated from the router with the lowest*
- *BGP router ID?*
- *Peer IP Address – Which route originated from the router with the*
- *lowest IP?*

When applying attributes, Weight and Local Preference are applied to inbound routes, dictating the best outbound path.

AS-Path and MED are applied to outbound routes, dictating the best inbound path.

23. Can we use local preference outside the autonomous system?

No, we can't, the reason is it is local and it is for within the AS. It can dictate the AS (our own) which path to take
LOCAL PREFERENCE is a very powerful attribute in BGP route selection. Local preference settings cannot be sent from one AS to another. AT&T allows the customer to send community strings according to RFC1998 (see Dynamic Customer Control) which trigger the setting of local preference for routes to the customer in the AT&T IP Backbone. Customer's should take care when using Local Preference, as it can force traffic into taking a very indirect, and possibly high latency route to reach a directly connected customer. For example, a local Preference of 70 will cause AT&T to use a peer connection to reach a directly connected customer if a route to that customer through the peer exists.

http://www.onesc.net/communities/as7018/

24. Does it require that BGP router-id should be reachable in cloud?

No, it is not required, if the router-id is advertised in IGP than it's possible otherwise not

25. What is recursive lookup in BGP and how it works?

When a packet forwards to the destination address the next hop address is checked and corresponding to that next hop address an outgoing interface is selected where the packet actually moves. Let's consider what happens when the routing table receives some prefixes with next hop loopback address of some router. In this case first a route lookup will be checked whether the destination prefix is in the routing table if yes then a lookup is performed for its next hop address because in this case next hop address is not directly connected interface. For latter , it will use the recursive lookup. This algorithm will work till it gets the directly connected interface. In most of the cases no recursive lookup will take more than 2 steps

26. What is the meaning of update source loopback?

The updates that are sent are sent via the loopback.

neighbor YY.YY.2.2 remote-as YY
neighbor YY.YY.2.2 update-source Loopback0
neighbor YY.YY.2.2 route-reflector-client

27. If a static route is advertised in BGP without using update source what will be the next hop address in update?

It depends on who you are advertising to. If it is advertised to iBGP neighbor, it uses the nexthop as it is in RIB table. If it is without nexthop in RIB, it will set the BGP source address.

28. Define various types of BGP communities and why they are used?

Two Types are communities are there
   a. **Extended** and
   b. **Standard**
And Standard has 4 types:
   1. no-advertise,
   2. no-export,
   3. local-as,
   4. internet

29. If BGP neighbor state is showing idle what does it meant

- Router is currently not attempting any connection establishment - The process has not yet started
- Establish means, BGP neighbors have been formed.

30. In Multihoming scenario if primary link gets fail, after how long traffic will be shifted to secondary link.

- By default, fast external failover is enabled for eBGP neighbor. So, when rsess interface fails, it immediately brings down the BGP session and next best path will be selected. if you have it disabled, it will rely on the BGP hold timer which 180 seconds (3 minutes)
- hold timer = 3 X keepalives(60)

31. I am having two routes for remote destination, but only single route is installing in routing table, what's the reason for this?

There could be many reasons for example;

- First next hop is not reachable
- Weigh attribute is higher, or AS is different ,
- Local PRE difference or MET different

32. How many links can be assigned for load balancing or sharing?

Two links

33. In beg I am establishing my neighborship with loopback address but it's not coming up.

Please specify different reasons for not coming up.

- Basic reason is Loopback reachability is not there with the neigh
- It can't be set to no synchronous

34. Can we redistribute BGP in IGPl? Please explain your answers n

of course, but we don't do it because BGP routing table is much bigger and router will crash as IGP is not supposed to handle it

35. What is BGP Route Reflector Cluster ID?

A router that is acting as a route reflector client does not require any specific configuration. It simply has fewer IBGP sessions than it would have if it were part of the full mesh. But improperly configuring the client to also be a reflector could easily cause a loop. An IBGP route coming in from one of the real reflectors to the client could be forwarded by the client, erroneously acting as reflector, to the other reflector.

Route reflector clusters prevent IBGP routing loops in redundant route reflector designs.

The role of the network designer is to properly identify which route reflectors and their clients will form a cluster. The designer assigns to the cluster a cluster-ID number that is unique within the AS.

Note The cluster-ID number must be configured in the route reflectors. The clients should not be configured with this information.

A route reflector router can reflect routes only within a single cluster. A route reflector can, however, participate in another cluster but only as a client. A client can function as a client only to a route reflector belonging to the same cluster
Route Reflector Cluster ID is a four-byte BGP attribute, and, by default, it is taken from the Route Reflector's BGP router ID. If two routers share the same BGP cluster ID, they belong to the same cluster. [4]

36. Why Cluster list it used?

Cluster list is used for loop prevention by only the route reflectors. Route reflector clients do not use cluster list attribute, so they do not know to which cluster they belong.

37. I am receiving updates from eBGP peer, will the next hop change or not?

- Yes, by default next-hop-self is done for
- IGP doesn't send it , BGP does send it

38. A router is receiving same route from two different eBGP peers. The AS information contains in peer 1 is {65500, 65550, 65555} and in peer 2 is {65501, 65501}. But I want to make peer 1 preferred.

Change LP, weight increase, AS path increase, community is for others

39. What is the difference between next-hop-self and update source loopback?

- route if next-hop-self is used changed to itself
- the routes are sent from loopback

This command is for advertising route direction. It is used in cases where the neighbor router doesn't know how to reach the advertising router, but the router with the next-hop-self-command does.

40. If I'm using the update-source loopback or next-hop-self commands, will they modify the source IP address in the packet?

They do not modify addresses on packets. The update-source command will try to form a neighbor relationship using an address different than the directly connected address, while the next-hop-self-command tells a neighbor where to send packets when the neighbor doesn't know how to reach the advertising router.

41. Define loop prevention mechanism in BGP.

If a route is revised with its own AS, it will drop the route
Can you force it? Yes, via command

42. What are IGPs and EGPs and why are they different?
Interior Gateway Protocols such as RIP, OSPF, IGRP, EIGRP and IS-IS are used within the network of a single organization or a part of an organization, Exterior Gateway Protocols such as EGP and BGP are used for routing between different organizations or "administrative domains".

43. What do BGP, eBGP, iBGP and AS stand for? What's the difference between eBGP and iBGP?
Border Gateway Protocol, internal BGP, external BGP, Autonomous System. eBGP is used towards other autonomous systems, iBGP is used within an AS.

44. What is the global routing table? What is (roughly) its size?
The global routing table is a list of all prefixes (and associated information) that are in use within the internet. Its size is approximately 130,000 prefixes currently.

45. Why is there a problem with iBGP in large networks? How can this problem be solved? Describe each solution in 1 - 3 sentences.

There must be a **full mesh of iBGP sessions**, in other words: each BGP router within an AS must have iBGP sessions with all other BGP routers in the AS. By requiring that all information in iBGP is learned directly from the router that learned the information over eBGP, there can't be any loops in iBGP. The full mesh requirement can be solved using either **route reflectors or confederations.**

46. Unlike all other routing protocols, BGP uses TCP as its transport protocol. Discuss the consequences of running BGP over UDP. (What would happen and/or what would have to be changed in BGP.)

In order to be able to run over UDP, BGP would have to implement functionality that is normally associated with transport protocols, such as retransmissions and reordering. Since in BGP communication is always with specific neighbors that are known in advance, using TCP here allows for a simpler implementation.

47. What are the disadvantages of existing and proposed BGP security mechanisms?

BGP TCP MD5 option: hard to implement on general purpose systems, hard to manage because password must match on both sides with no provisions for setting up/changing it, only protects session between two routers, information in BGP may still be wrong.

S-BGP and soBGP: currently, there is no repository of known prefix-to-AS mappings that these protocols could secure. Experience with cryptographic authentication shows there are regularly mistakes that lead to information that is valid being rejected because of a problem with the authentication.

S-BGP: the amount of extra memory in routers and the number of signature checks can be problematic for existing routers, and offloading isn't possible. Secret key must be stored on the router to be able to generate signatures.

48. Suppose AS 10 is a multihomed customer of AS 20 and AS 30. AS 10 receives most of its incoming traffic over AS 30 and wants to employ traffic engineering techniques to shift some of this traffic from AS 30 to AS 20. For this purpose, a route map is created. Assume that the following excerpt of the BGP table is a good representation of the BGP table as a whole:

```
   Network           Next Hop        Metric LocPrf Weight Path
*>i12.31.126.0/24    213.24.40.91       0    100      0 20 209 13606 i
*                    62.93.19.27        0             0 30 209 13606 i
*  i12.31.127.0/24   213.24.40.91       0    100      0 20 209 7018 23087 i
*>                   62.93.19.27        0             0 30 7018 23087 i
*  i12.31.159.0/24   213.24.40.91       0    100      0 20 209 7018 20457 i
*>                   62.93.19.27        0             0 30 4181 20457 i
```

Questions:

a. Which BGP attributes would AS 10 possibly like to change in the route map "set" clause, in what way (higher/lower, longer/shorter), and which would be the best choice?

Answer:

The only real option for influencing incoming traffic is to make the AS path longer as local preference and MED metric aren't communicated to the source AS. [5]

b. **8b. Should a "match" clause be used in this route map?**
Answer
No, that's not necessary as we want to apply the change to all outgoing routing information.

c. **Should the route map be applied to?**
The BGP session with AS 20 "in"
The BGP session with AS 20 "out"
The BGP session with AS 30 "in"
The BGP session with AS 30 "out"
Answer
The path over AS 30 as seen by remote ASes must become longer, so the route map must be applied to the session with AS 30 for "out".

49. What is the function of the connection collision detection mechanism?
Because both BGP routers may try to open a session to the other at the same time, it is possible that two sessions are established at the same time. The connection collision detection

mechanism detects this situation and then applies a set of rules to determine which of the two sessions is terminated and which one is actually used.

50. What is the "longest match first" rule and what does it do? (Provide an example if necessary.)

When two overlapping prefixes are present in the routing table, an address that falls within the overlapping range will match the longest of these prefixes (= the smallest block of addresses or the "more specific" prefix). For instance, 10.0.1.1 matches both 10.0.0.0/8 (which is 10.0.0.0 - 10.255.255.255) and 10.0.1.0/24 (which is 10.0.1.0 - 10.0.1.255). **The second prefix is more specific**: it has a prefix length of 24 while the first prefix has a length of 8. So, when looking in the routing table to see where a packet with address 10.0.1.1 should go, the match will be 10.0.1.0/24.

51. What is the version of BGP that first supported CIDR?
   a. BGP version 1
   b. BGP version 2
   c. BGP version 3
   d. BGP version 4
   e. BGP version 5
   f. None of the above

   Answer d

52. What are valid BGP terms? (Multiple answers are possible.)
   a. **Communities**
   b. Conglomerates
   c. Confederations
   d. Corporations
   e. None of the above

   Answer C
   communities are used to tag BGP routes so upstream routers (within the same or a different AS) may take special actions for this route. Confederations use multiple AS numbers internally, but present only a single AS to the rest of the world. This makes it possible to have many BGP routers in an AS without needing an iBGP connection between every pair.

53. On top of which protocol does BGP run?
   a. Directly on top of IP
   b. UDP
   c. TCP
   d. None of the above

   Answer C

54. The Cisco IOS "no synchronization" configuration option is used to disable synchronization between BGP and the IGP, so there is no need to add it to the configuration under the following circumstances:

   a. Never, it is the default
   b. When you're running an IGP, because then you'll want to synchronize
   c. When you're not running an IGP, because there is no need

d. **None of the above**

the correct answer is "None of the above", because:
- the default is to synchronize
- running an IGP does not necessarily mean you want to synchronize
- when you're not running an IGP you must turn of synchronization, otherwise iBGP won't work

55. MBGP means:
   a.   Multilink BGP
   b.   **Multiprotocol BGP**
   c.   Multicast BGP
   d.   None of the above

The answer is **Multiprotocol BGP**. MBGP is used to propagate multicast and IPv6 routing information.

Multiprotocol BGP. MBGP is used to propagate multicast and IPv6 routing information.

56. In the global routing table, sometimes the same AS number shows up more than once in a path.
   Yes
   No

The correct answer is **"Yes"**. This happens because some ASes inject their AS number in the path more than once. In the absence of AS path prepending, every AS number should only show up once, because BGP doesn't allow looping AS paths.

57. When ARIN, RIPE or the APNIC assigns you the range 221.30.48.0 - 221.30.50.255 out of a 221.30.48.0 - 221.30.63.255 allocation, you should announce over BGP:
   Three /24's
   A /23 and a /24
   A /22
   A /20
   A /19
   None of the above

Answer is **A /20** provides for optimal route aggregation and stability.

58. What would you say to someone who wants to run BGP on a Cisco 2500 router (check all that apply):
   a.   **There is no software image that supports BGP for the 2500** (no need to check other answers)
   b.   That won't work, a 2500 is too slow
   c.   You don't want this, a 2500 is too slow
   d.   That will work if you don't take full routing from your peers
   e.   That will work, even with full routing
   f.   None of the above

Answer: a
"a" Cisco 2500 can run BGP. The router won't hold a full BGP table, but this is certainly not always a necessity. Also, processing a large amount of routing information takes a long time, but it does work.

59. Local preference is:

a. Local to a single router
b. **Local to a single AS**
c. Local to a single neighbor connection
d. None of the above
Answer: b
local preference is local to a single AS. The local preference is communicated over iBGP but not over eBGP.

60. When selecting the best path, the BGP protocol takes into account the following information in the stated order:

a. Path, origin type, multi-exit discriminator, local preference
b. Path, origin type, local preference, multi-exit discriminator
c. **Local preference, path, origin type, multi-exit discriminator**
d. Local preference, path, multi-exit discriminator, origin type
e. None of the above
Answer c

10. MPLS

After IGP and BGP questions, I prepared basic list of MPLS interview questions which could help you to clear your next level.

A. BASIC MPLS

MPLS is an acronym for Multiprotocol Label Switching which is a type of data-carrying technique for high-performance telecommunications networks. MPLS is the most widely used technology in Internet Service Providers and Telecom Networks all over the world.

MPLS directs data from one network node to the next based on short path labels rather than long network addresses, avoiding complex look-ups in a routing table.

MPLS is also called Layer 2.5 as it resides between Layer 2 and Layer 3 of the OSI layer model.

Highlight: MPLS is called Multiprotocol because it can carry anything over an MPLS path irrespective of the underlying protocol: Ethernet, ATM, PPP, SONET etc. This behavior is known as AToM i.e. Any Transport over MPLS.

MPLS Terminologies:

Label: It is a 32-bit field that is locally significant and is used to represent an FEC of a packet.

Label numbers ranging from 0 to 15 are reserved labels and can only be used for special purposes. They cannot be used by an LSR for normal forwarding. Each reserved label has its own specific function such as Label 3 is the implicit NULL label whereas Label 14 is OAM alert label, and so on and so forth. [6]

1. **What is the difference between VPN and MPLS?**
   VPN, also known as Virtual Private Network, is basically a virtual network within a physical network. It is generally deployed to be high security network tunnel through which data travels in a strongly encrypted form. Thus, any data travelling over a VPN is not visible to the physical network surrounding it.

   MPLS is short for Multi-Protocol Label Switching, which is a protocol that uses labels to route packets instead of using IP addresses. It is a technology directs and carries data between network nodes, which means it's possible to create direct virtual links between different nodes regardless of locations and distances.

2. **What is MPLS and why it is being so popular in short time?**

   MPLS is multi-protocol label switching mechanism which uses the label to forward the traffic to the next hop address. It is popular because it must be used for CPN (Converge Packet Network).

3. What is the protocol used by MPLS?

MPLS uses TDP or LDP.

4. MPLS works on which layer?

MPLS works between layer 2 and layer 3, sometimes it is called 2.5 layer protocol.

5. What is the difference between P and PE router?

P router doesn't have Customer network routes where in PE router is having customer network routes. Another reason is P router doesn't require MP-iBGP but for PE it is must.

6. Can I make my PE router as P?

To make your PE router as P, you need to remove the BGP configurations and after that it will not participate with customer network.

7. Two routers are having 4 equal cost links, how many LDP sessions will be established?

One session

8. My LDP router id, OSPF router id and BGP router id is different, will it work to forward the traffic of customers or not?

LDP router id and BGP router-id should be same if SP is using labels only for loopbacks. If labels are generated for each and every route then no problem at all.

9. What is Penultimate Hop Popping and why it is required? Which router performs the PHP function?

Second last router performs the Penultimate Hop Popping function to remove the top most label.

10. I am receiving aggregate label, what does it mean?

It is important to understand the sequence information about MPLS. MPLS uses label switching to forward packets over Ethernet. Labels are assigned to packets based on groupings or forwarding equivalence classes (FECs). The label is added between the Layer 2 and the Layer 3 header.

In an MPLS network, the label edge router (LER) performs a label lookup of the incoming label, swaps the incoming label with an outgoing label, and sends the packet to the next hop at the label switch router (LSR). Labels are imposed (pushed) on packets only at the ingress edge of the MPLS network and are removed (popped) at the egress edge. The core network LSRs (provider, or P routers) read the labels, apply the appropriate services, and forward the packets based on the labels.

Incoming labels are aggregate or nonaggregate. The aggregate label indicates that the arriving MPLS packet must be switched through an IP lookup to find the next hop and the outgoing interface. The nonaggregate label indicates that the packet contains the IP next hop information.

11. **What are the different types of labels?**

    Implicit Null, Explicit Null, Aggregate Label etc.

12. **How to make customer route unique?**

    Using Route distinguisher, you can make the customer unique

13. **What is the difference between RD and RT?**

    RD is not an extended community where as RT is an extended community.

14. **Can I assign a same RD to two different customers?**

    No, you shouldn't; assigning the same RD means they will exchange their routes, so if they are different customers, we don't want them to learn other routes.
    But if we want to import the routes or subset of routes between the two customers, how do we do that?
    Using Route targets, same routing targets on both customers

15. **Does RD travels in route update?**

    No

16. **My customer is having three branches and all are attached to three different PEs, In this case can I use the different vrf names?**

    Yes

17. **What is downstream on demand?**

    Downstream router is the one which is responsible to advertise the label first to upstream router in case of downstream on demand method is selected.
    Upstream router is the one which advertise the labels to its downstream router after receiving label bindings from it.

18. **How to filter MPLS labels?**

    By using ACLs.

19. **What is the default range of MPLS labels in Cisco routers? How to extend that range?**

    16 – 100000 is default range

20. **Without BGP / mp-bgp can I implement MPLS?**

21. **Without route reflector can I implement MPLS?**

    Yes, need to develop full mesh BGP

22. **What is the difference between VPNv4 and IPv4 address family?**

We always accept and forward IP packets to customers, for this we need to use ipv4 address-family. When the customers packets are being received by PE they become labeled one and to forward labeled packets to different PE/RR; address-family vpnv4 is required. In short we can say that ipv4 address-family is being used for customers and vpnv4 address-family is used by SP core.

23. What is MP-iBGP? Can we use normal BGP in lieu of MP-iBGP?

No, MP-iBGP is used because of the support of multi-protocol which normal BGP doesn't support.

24. What is LIB, LFIB?

LIB – Label Information Base.
The LIB is an MPLS table. This is the place where the router will keep all known MPLS labels. To take a look, you just need to use show mpls ldp bindings.

LFIB – Label Forwarding Instance Base.
The LFIB is another MPLS table. This is the table that the router uses to forward labelled packets going through the network. Much like the RIB uses the FIB to forward traffic, so the LIB uses the LFIB to forward traffic.

25. What is CEF and without enabling CEF, can we make MPLS work?

CEF is mandatory in Cisco routers for MPLS.

26. I am receiving end to end customer routes on various PE but not able to ping those routes, what could be the problem?

LDP is not configured in the path.

27. What is explicit null and implicit null?

Both implicit and explicit null labels are generated by last hop router to its neighbors. Implicit null is by default which means penultimate router should only send IP packet thus it pops the label (popping the label known as PHP and this is done to reduce the load on last hop router). The one disadvantage in implicit null approach is if the network is configured for QoS based on MPLS EXP bits, then QoS is lost between penultimate router and last hop router.

In this case, we can make use of explicit null which means penultimate hop router does not pop the label. It sends with label value of 0 but with other fields including EXP bits intact. This way QoS treatment is preserved between penultimate router and last hop router. Explicit null should be configured manually in last hop router.

28. Does LDP require OSPF, IS-IS or BGP?

NO, it is not necessary, MPLS support any kind of routing protocols. And the basic task of LDP is to perform main 3 action on the router,

1) Push the label
2) Swap the label
3) Pop the label

Note: MPLS is used for multiprotocol.

29. In neighbor discovery command, I am receiving only xmit, what does it mean?
At another end MPLS IP is not configured.
30. What is transport address?

Route id is transport address

31. What is the RFC of MPLS?

RFC 3031 MPLS Architecture January 2001 MPLS stands for "Multiprotocol" Label Switching, multiprotocol because its techniques are applicable to ANY network layer protocol

For more information about RFC of MPLS in different application we can see in the below list.

o   RFC 2547, BGP/MPLS VPNs
o   RFC 2702, Requirements for Traffic Engineering Over MPLS
o   RFC 2858, Multiprotocol Extensions for BGP-4
o   RFC 3031, Multiprotocol Label Switching Architecture
o   RFC 3032, MPLS Label Stack Encoding
o   RFC 3063, MPLS Loop Prevention Mechanism
o   RFC 3140, Per Hop Behavior Identification Codes
o   RFC 3270, Multi-Protocol Label Switching (MPLS) Support of Differentiated Services (E-LSPs only)
o   RFC 3443, Time To Live (TTL) Processing in Multi-Protocol Label Switching (MPLS) Networks
o   RFC 3469, Framework for Multi-Protocol Label Switching (MPLS)-based Recovery
o   RFC 3564, Requirements for Support of Differentiated Services-aware MPLS Traffic Engineering
o   RFC 4124, Protocol Extensions for Support of Diffserv-aware MPLS Traffic Engineering
o   RFC 4125, Maximum Allocation Bandwidth Constraints Model for Diffserv-aware MPLS Traffic Engineering
o   RFC 4127, Russian Dolls Bandwidth Constraints Model for Diffserv-aware MPLS Traffic Engineering
o   RFC 4379, Detecting Multi-Protocol Label Switched (MPLS) Data Plane Failures.
o   RFC 3815, Definitions of Managed Objects for the Multiprotocol Label Switching (MPLS), Label Distribution Protocol (LDP)
o   RFC 4448, Encapsulation Methods for Transport of Ethernet over MPLS Networks
o   RFC 5462, Multiprotocol Label Switching (MPLS) Label Stack Entry: "EXP" Field Renamed to "Traffic Class" Field.

32. Why MPLS is called multi-protocol?
MPLS is called multiprotocol because it works with the Internet Protocol (IP), Asynchronous Transport Mode (ATM), and frame relay network protocols. The advantage of MPLS is that it

eliminates multiple routers, firewalls and IT management headaches from all of the remote locations.

33. What is the difference between MPLS, SSL and IPsec?

MPLS and IPSEC VPN's offer many of the same features and functionality. The choice of whether or not to use MPLS or IPSEC VPN's is dependent upon the size of the deployment and the reach of the providers offering the service. Management and cost are significant factors that must be evaluated.

34. I am using different vendor products and want to implement TDP, what type of challenges will you face?

TDP (Tag Distribution Protocol) is a Cisco's proprietary protocol. Cisco created a protocol and a standard was created later. This is exactly how some of the other standard protocols were developed such as 802.1Q/ISL or PaGP/LACP. TDP is now entirely replaced with LDP hence no one should be implementing TDP and instead implement/use LDP (Label Distribution Protocol).

35. Does MPLS support IPv6?

MPLS does not support IPv6. However, Before the IPv6 Provider Edge Router over MPLS (6PE) feature can be implemented, MPLS must be running over the core IPv4 network. If Cisco routers are used, Cisco Express Forwarding or distributed Cisco Express Forwarding must be enabled for both IPv4 and IPv6 protocols.

36. Can I use the existing IPv4 MPLS backbone for IPv6?
Existing IPv4 MPLS backbone can be used for IPv6 using tunnels; you can do that by creating tunnels and then enable ipv6 routing through this tunnel. IPv6 traffic will encapsulate in IPv4 header and router will see it as ipv4 traffic.

37. What is adjacency table?

The adjacency table maintains layer 2 or switching information linked to a particular FIB entry, avoiding the need for an Address Resolution Protocol (ARP) request for each table lookup.

38. What is MPLS-TP?

The Multiprotocol Label Switching Transport Profile (MPLS-TP) is an extension of Multiprotocol Label Switching (MPLS), the protocol that allows most packets to be forwarded at the Layer 2 (switching) level rather than at the Layer 3 (routing) level. MPLS-TP is designed to speed up and shape network traffic in telecommunications transport networks.

39. Define various Cisco troubleshooting commands in MPLS?

Important troubleshooting commands are defined in the following table.

Purpose of troubleshooting Commands	Commands
Check the MPLS LDP peer table on router	[R1] disp mpls ldp peer
Check whether LDP protocol is enabled	[R1] disp mpls ldp peer
Check whether MPLS is enabled on the interface	[R1] disp mpls interface
Check whether LDP is enabled on the interface.	[R1] disp mpls ldp interface
Check the MPLS configuration to verify the MPLS configuration on Router.	[R] disp current-configuration | begin mpls
Check whether LSR-ID is distinct on both routers.	[R1] disp mpls ldp peer
Check LDP session established between Routers	[R1] disp mpls ldp session
Configure the command lsp-trigger all under MPLS view	[R1]-mpls]lsp-trigger all
Check the ip-prefix configured on R1.	[R1] disp ip ip-prefix
We can reset mpls ldp on R1.	[R1] reset mpls ldp
Verify the vpn peer table.	[R1] disp bgp vpnv4 vpn-instance vpn1 pe
Check the IBGP peer relation between router.	[R1] disp bgp peer
Check the OSPF configuration on router.	[R1] disp current-configuration | begin ospf
Check the routing table for vpn-instance vpn1 on Router R1.	[R1] disp ip routing-table vpn-instance vpn1
Verify the status of tunnel	[R1] disp mpls te tunnel
Verify the tunnel path	[R1] disp mpls te tunnel path
The debug mpls packets command	[R1] Debug mpls packets
show the detail of forwarding table	[R1] show mpls forwarding- table detail
To display the status of the TDP discovery process	[R1] show tag-switching tdp discovery

Table 14 Troubleshooting commands in MPLS

40. What is forward equivalence class aka FEC?

A forwarding equivalence class (FEC) is a term used in Multiprotocol Label Switching (MPLS) to describe a set of packets with similar or identical characteristics which may be forwarded the same way; that is, they may be bound to the same MPLS label.

Characteristics determining the FEC of a higher-layer packet depend on the configuration of the router, but typically this is at least the destination IP address. Quality of service class is also often used. Thus, a forward equivalence class tends to correspond to a label switched path (LSP). The reverse is not true, however: an LSP may be (and usually is) used for multiple FECs.

41. Difference between MPLS IP and MPLS Label Protocol LDP command?

MPLS IP command
To enable Multiprotocol Label Switching (MPLS) forwarding of IPv4 and IPv6 packets along normally routed paths for a particular interface, we use the mpls ip command in interface configuration mode. To disable this configuration, use the no form of this command. [8]
> **mpls ip**
> **no mpls ip**

The following example shows how to enable label switching on the specified Ethernet interface:

> **Switch(config)# configure terminal**
> **Switch(config-if)# interface TenGigabitEthernet1/0/3**
> **Switch(config-if)# mpls ip**

The following example shows that label switching is enabled on the specified vlan interface (SVI)

> on a Cisco Catalyst switch:
> **Switch(config)# configure terminal**
> **Switch(config-if)# interface vlan 1**
> **Switch(config-if)#**   **mpls**   **ip**

MPLS Label Distribution Protocol (LDP) command

To specify the label distribution protocol for an interface, use the mpls label protocol command in interface configuration mode. To remove the label distribution protocol from the interface, use the no form of this command.

> **mpls label protocol ldp**
> **no mpls label protocol ldp.**

The following command establishes LDP as the label distribution protocol for the platform:
> **Switch(config)# mpls label protocol ldp**

42. If MPLS get disable, will it harm my IGP or IPv4 traffic?

Disabling MPLS doesn't harm the regular IPv4 traffic; it will instead be routed using routing table.

43. What is downstream and upstream router in MPLS?
Downstream router is the one which is responsible to advertise the label first to upstream router in case of downstream on demand method is selected.
Upstream router is the one which advertise the labels to its downstream router after receiving label bindings from it. [9]

44. Difference between MPLS and MPLS-TP?

Already explained above

45. How does LDP Initializes?

Highest loopback id starts the Label Distribution Protocol initialization process by sending common session parameter TLV which includes a sub TLV of parameters containing session protocol version, session keepalive time, advertisement method, loop detection and session path vector. In the given diagram, I have started MPLS LDP firstly on 100.100.100.1 (R1) and 100.100.100.2(R2). So, in this case R2 send a first initialization message to R1 by adding all the above TLV parameters.

The following figure show the LDP initialization process.

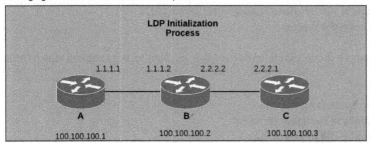

Figure 19 LDP Initialization Process

Structure of LDP initialization message sent from R2 to R1.

```
⊟ Label Distribution Protocol
    version: 1
    PDU Length: 32
    LSR ID: 100.100.100.2 (100.100.100.2)
    Label Space ID: 0
  ⊟ Initialization Message
      0... .... = U bit: Unknown bit not set
      Message Type: Initialization Message (0x200)
      Message Length: 22
      Message ID: 0x00000001
    ⊟ Common Session Parameters TLV
        00.. .... = TLV Unknown bits: Known TLV, do not Forward (0x00)
        TLV Type: Common Session Parameters TLV (0x500)
        TLV Length: 14
      ⊟ Parameters
          Session Protocol version: 1
          Session KeepAlive Time: 180
          0... .... = Session Label Advertisement Discipline: Downstream Unsolicited proposed
          .0.. .... = Session Loop Detection: Loop Detection Disabled
          Session Path vector Limit: 0
```

Being R2 is having highest LDP router id, so it starts sending the label information to R1. We can say R2 is working as downstream LSR to R1. R2 sending Address message and label mapping message which are sub part of label distribution protocol.

```
⊟ Label Distribution Protocol
    version: 1
    PDU Length: 172
    LSR ID: 100.100.100.2 (100.100.100.2)
    Label Space ID: 0
  ⊞ Address Message
  ⊞ Label Mapping Message
  ⊞ Label Mapping Message
  ⊞ Label Mapping Message
  ⊞ Label Mapping Message
  ⊞ Label Mapping Message
```

Address message is only containing the directly connected interface IP address of R2 which are 1.1.1.2, 2.2.2.2 and 100.100.100.2.

```
⊟ Label Distribution Protocol
    version: 1
    PDU Length: 172
    LSR ID: 100.100.100.2 (100.100.100.2)
    Label Space ID: 0
  ⊟ Address Message
      0... .... = U bit: unknown bit not set
      Message Type: Address Message (0x300)
      Message Length: 22
      Message ID: 0x00000003
    ⊟ Address List TLV
        00.. .... = TLV unknown bits: Known TLV, do not Forward (0x00)
        TLV Type: Address List TLV (0x101)
        TLV Length: 14
        Address Family: IPv4 (1)
      ⊟ Addresses
          Address 1: 1.1.1.2
          Address 2: 2.2.2.2
          Address 3: 100.100.100.2
  ⊞ Label Mapping Message
```

Along with this R2 is also sending label mapping message which is containing the information about route, label and address family. Address family means whether it is ipv4 route or vpnv4 route. R2 is sending an information about 1.1.1.0 prefix by including label 3 which is used for PHP (Penultimate Hop Popping).

```
⊟ Label Mapping Message
    0... .... = U bit: unknown bit not set
    Message Type: Label Mapping Message (0x400)
    Message Length: 24
    Message ID: 0x00000004
  ⊟ Forwarding Equivalence Classes TLV
      00.. .... = TLV unknown bits: Known TLV, do not Forward (0x00)
      TLV Type: Forwarding Equivalence Classes TLV (0x100)
      TLV Length: 8
    ⊟ FEC Elements
      ⊟ FEC Element 1
          FEC Element Type: Prefix FEC (2)
          FEC Element Address Type: IPv4 (1)
          FEC Element Length: 30
          Prefix: 1.1.1.0
  ⊟ Generic Label TLV
      00.. .... = TLV unknown bits: Known TLV, do not Forward (0x00)
      TLV Type: Generic Label TLV (0x200)
      TLV Length: 4
      Generic Label: 3
```

The same way R2 is sending a label 16 to R1 for 100.100.100.1 which is loopback address of R1 itself and label 16 becomes as local label in R2 forwarding table.

```
⊟ Label Mapping Message
     0... .... = U bit: Unknown bit not set
     Message Type: Label Mapping Message (0x400)
     Message Length: 24
     Message ID: 0x00000006
  ⊟ Forwarding Equivalence Classes TLV
     00.. .... = TLV Unknown bits: Known TLV, do not Forward (0x00)
     TLV Type: Forwarding Equivalence Classes TLV (0x100)
     TLV Length: 8
   ⊟ FEC Elements
     ⊟ FEC Element 1
        FEC Element Type: Prefix FEC (2)
        FEC Element Address Type: IPv4 (1)
        FEC Element Length: 32
        Prefix: 100.100.100.1
  ⊟ Generic Label TLV
     00.. .... = TLV Unknown bits: Known TLV, do not Forward (0x00)
     TLV Type: Generic Label TLV (0x200)
     TLV Length: 4
     Generic Label: 16
```

```
R2#show mpls fo
R2#show mpls forwarding-table
Local  Outgoing    Prefix          Bytes tag  Outgoing    Next Hop
tag    tag or VC   or Tunnel Id    switched   interface
16     Pop tag     100.100.100.1/32  0        Fa0/0       1.1.1.1
17     Pop tag     100.100.100.3/32  0        Fa0/1       2.2.2.1
```

Once this is done then R1 initiates a label mapping process by sending the label and FEC information to R2 (R2 is upstream LSR to R1).

After this, R3 is started which is having loopback address of 100.100.100.3. In this case R3 will start the initialization process of LDP being R3 is having highest LDP router id.

Now R3 becomes downstream LSR to R2 and R2 becomes upstream LSR to R3. Once R3 will exchange all the label mappings then R2 will initiate the process and send the information to R3.

Now how the updates of new route will flood. To test this, a new route 100.100.100.100 is installed in R3. After this we saw a label mapping message was sent from 100.100.100.2 to 100.100.100.1 and vice versa but the communication was being started by 100.100.100.2

[10]

46. What is Cell Mode MPLS over ATM?

Basically, cell-mode ATM is an MPLS implementation which uses native ATM tagging mechanism for label switching.

47. Difference Between VC Based Multiplexing and Logical Link Control Encapsulation in ATM?

VC based Multiplexing (AAL5Mux) is used to carry one protocol per PVC. e.g. If we want to forward IP and IPX over ATM, in this case we need to define two dedicated PVC. One PVC will carry IP and another will carry IPX. As the number of protocols will increase, PVC will also increase.

Logical Link Control Encapsulation (AAL5Snap) is used to carry multiple protocols in single PVC. In this case user multiplexes all the protocols in one PVC.

48. Basics of ATM?

Asynchronous transfer mode (ATM) is a switching technique used by telecommunication networks that uses asynchronous time-division multiplexing to encode data into small, fixed-sized cells. ATM is the core protocol used over the synchronous optical network (SONET) backbone of the integrated digital services network (ISDN).

49. ATM is packet or circuit switching?

ATM provides functionality that is similar to both circuit switching and packet switching networks: ATM uses asynchronous time-division multiplexing, and encodes data into small, fixed-sized packets (ISO-OSI frames) called cells.

50. Is LDP Required for VPNv4 Labels?

In case of layer 3 VPN, two labels are normally carried by packet. But the differentiation between the labels is ipv4 and vpnv4. Ipv4 label is used for IGP and vpnv4 label is used for customer route. Normally a question comes in mind, "Is LDP responsible for both the labels". The answer is no because LDP is only responsible for the top most label is IGP label and MP-iBGP is responsible for vpnv4 label which is present under beneath of IGP label. Even if the core network is not running LDP, but MP-iBGP is enabled from PE to PE, we can easily see the vpnv4 labels exchange. But the problem is that traffic forwarding will not happen because the core network doesn't understand the labels. [11]

51. What will happen if you see your PE loopback in vpnv4 table?

May be the next time you will be weird to see your PE loopback address in VPNv4 routing table. The first thought which comes in mind that how my PE loopback can be part of the VPNv4 routing table because this is the table which actually contains the information of all the VRFs. Is your PE is working as VRF? No, not at all then what's the reason behind this.

Check the given output which I captured from the RR server.
show ip bgp vpnv4 all | i 10.10.254.197 (10.10.254.197 is PE loopback address)
          *>i10.169.68.0/24 10.10.254.197 0 100 0 ?
          *>i10.235.10.8/30 10.10.254.197 0 100 0 ?
          *>i10.16.190.8/30 10.10.254.197 0 100 0 ?
          *>i10.80.85.128/25 10.10.254.197 0 100 0 ?
          *>i10.80.97.0/26 10.10.254.197 0 100 0 ?
          *>i10.235.24.8/30 10.10.254.197 0 100 0 ?
          *>i10.235.54.8/30 10.10.254.197 0 100 0 ?

```
*  i10.176.1.40/30 10.10.254.197 0 100 0 ?
*  i10.176.2.0/30 10.10.254.197 0 100 0 ?
*>i10.179.32.0/26 10.10.254.197 0 100 0 ?
*>i10.103.66.48/28 10.10.254.197 0 100 0 ?
*>i10.10.254.197/32 10.10.254.197 0 100 0 ?
```

You can see all the routes are getting with next-hop as PE address. But In the last line you can check the loopback entry is coming as VPNv4 route entry. Actually, it should not come. Now the next question comes in mind may be loopback is redistributed in BGP, Go and check you will find it is advertised in IGP not in BGP.

After that I logged in PE router i.e. 10.10.254.197 and ran given the command

PE-Router# **show ip bgp vpnv4 all**
BGP table version is 176194, local router ID is 10.10.254.197
Status codes: s suppressed, d damped, h history, * valid, > best, i - internal,
r RIB-failure, S Stale
Origin codes: i - IGP, e - EGP, ? - incomplete

```
Network Next Hop Metric LocPrf Weight Path
Route Distinguisher: 6x500:100
        *> 10.235.2.8/30 0.0.0.0 0 32768 ?
        *>i10.235.5.0/30 124.247.255.241 0 100 0 ?
        *>i10.235.5.4/30 124.247.255.241 0 100 0 ?
        *> 10.235.5.8/30 0.0.0.0 0 32768 ?
        Route Distinguisher: 6x000:123
        *>i0.0.0.0 10.10.254.205 10 100 0 ?
        *>i10.240.5.0/30 10.10.254.205 10 100 0 ?
        Route Distinguisher: 6x500:24
        *>i10.235.1.0/24 10.10.254.1 0 100 0 ?
        *>i10.235.1.32/30 10.10.254.1 0 100 0 ?
        Route Distinguisher: 6x500:640*>i0.0.0.0 10.10.254.20 0 100 0 ?
        *>i17.12.13.11/32 10.10.253.1 0 100 0 ?
        Route Distinguisher: 2:6x500:100
        *> 10.10.254.197/32 0.0.0.0 0 ?
        *>i14.47.255.241/32 14.47.255.241 0 100 0 ?
```

In the above output you can see the last route distinguisher which is 2:6x500:100 explicitly showing 10.10.254.197 is locally originate route and automatically it is binding new RD. This RD is something different from others because it is carrying 2 which explicitly states that it is mdt safi or used for your MVPN traffic. After that I checked RD 6x500:100 which is actually binding to a vrf which is using multicasting. Now check there is one more route which is 14.47.255.241/32. I did the telnet and checked what's belong to this route. Then I found a weird thing that the same MVPN client was configured on the router and 14.47.255.241 was the loopback address of the router.

By doing the above exercise I came to know two important things
1) From RR we can get total number of MVPN clients running on particular PE.
2) From particular PE we can fetch the information that where that particular MVPN is actually working.

You can do one more thing on RR check the "show ip bgp vpnv4 all" output of that PE where no MVPN is configured. In the output you will not get PE loopback address.

52. What is Bidirectional Forwarding Detection? BFD

BFD provides a low-overhead, short-duration method of detecting failures in the forwarding path between two adjacent routers, including the interfaces, data links, and forwarding planes. BFD is a detection protocol that you enable at the interface and routing protocol levels.

Cisco supports the BFD asynchronous mode, which depends on the sending of BFD control packets between two systems to activate and maintain BFD neighbor sessions between routers. Therefore, in order for a BFD session to be created, you must configure BFD on both systems (and BFD peers). Once BFD has been enabled on the interfaces and at the router level for the appropriate routing protocols, a BFD session is created, BFD timers are negotiated, and the BFD peers will begin to send BFD control packets to each other at the negotiated interval. BFD provides fast BFD peer failure detection times independently of all media types, encapsulations, topologies, and routing protocols BGP, EIGRP, IS-IS, and OSPF. By sending rapid failure detection notices to the routing protocols in the local router to initiate the routing table recalculation process, BFD Bidirectional Forwarding Detection Information About Bidirectional Forwarding Detection 4 Cisco IOS Release: Multiple Releases contributes to greatly reduced overall network convergence time.

53. Different types of PseudoWire?

Pseudowire emulation aka PWE3 that emulates the attributes of service over packet switched network (PSN). Pseudo means no physical existence only virtual. By using pseudowire, service provider can emulate any circuit end to end. E.g. if customer is looking for TDM bandwidth end to end, but SP is having a packet core network but no TDM backhaul, in that case pseudowire help SP to deliver end to end circuit which uses packet core network and provide TDM drop to customers. This is the case where in both termination points are having same output but in case of different output like one side Ethernet and another side frame-relay or atm, the best is to provision inter network circuit.
a pseudowire (PW) is a mechanism to tunnel traffic through a PSN
PWs are usually bidirectional (unlike MPLS LSPs)
PW architecture is an extension of VPN architecture

Types of Pseudowire

1. CESoPSN:- Circuit Emulation over Packer Switched Network supports framed and channelized TDM services over packet switched network.
2. SAToP:- Structure Agnostic TDM over Packet, is a TDM Pseudowire technology which treats the TDM traffic as data traffic and ignore the framing bits. It supports unframed TDM services.

Advantages of SAToP:-

1. Flexible packet size.
2. Lowest end to end delay.
3. Low overhead.

Advantages of CESoPSN:-

1. Lower packetization delay.

54. Modes of EoMPLS (Ethernet over MPLS)

Introduction

An Ethernet Pseudowire allows Ethernet packets to transport over MPLS cloud. By using this service customers simply extend their local area networks without losing the information. The spanning tree will work and end to end connectivity will be on same subnet. Other words, we can say it a virtual leased circuit. Customer end to end connectivity is aka as Emulated Service which operates over Pseudowire which further operates over Packet Switched Network (MPLS Network). Entire end to end communication reference model is depicted below.

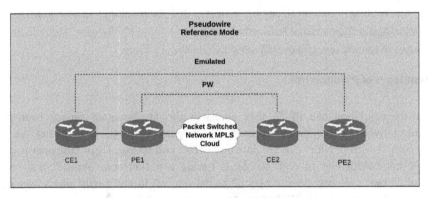

Figure 20 Ethernet Pseudowire

Modes of Ethernet Pseudowire

An Ethernet Pseudowire operates in two modes: raw mode and tagged mode. In tagged mode, each frame must have 802.1q tag and that tag is meaningful to the local and end point router. It should be noted that if the VLAN identifier is modified by the egress PE, the Ethernet spanning tree protocol might fail to work properly. If this issue is of significance, the VLAN identifier MUST be selected in such a way that it matches on the attachment circuits at both ends of the PW. It means the identifier or vlan tag should be used same not different. This mode use Pseudowire type 0x0004. Every frame sent on the PW must have a service-delimiting VLAN tag (Different vlans for different customers). If the frame as received by the PE from the attachment circuit does not have a service-delimiting VLAN tag, the PE must prepend the frame with a dummy VLAN tag before sending the frame on the PW.

But in case of raw mode, tag may or may not be added in the frame and is not meaning to the end points. Though the frame is forwarded transparently. This service corresponds to PW type

0x0005. If an Ethernet PW is operating in raw mode, service-delimiting tags are NEVER sent over the PW. If a service-delimiting tag is present when the frame is received from the attachment circuit by the PE, it must be stripped from the frame before the frame is sent to the PW.

55. What is the difference between MPLS and VPN?

    a. VPN is a network layered on top of a computer network; MPLS directs and carries data from one network node to the next.

    b. VPN use cryptographic tunneling protocols to provide high level security; MPLS is operable between the Data Link Layer and the Network Layer.

56. What is MPLS VPN? Why we use MPLS VPN.

One of the most popular of the MPLS applications is called MPLS virtual private networks (VPNs). MPLS VPN is a method of creating a Virtual Private Network (VPN) using Multi-Protocol Label Switching (MPLS). MPLS VPNs allow a service provider, or even a large enterprise, to offer Layer 3 VPN services. In particular, SPs oftentimes replace older Layer 2 WAN services such as Frame Relay and ATM with an MPLS VPN service. MPLS VPN services enable the possibility for the SP to provide a wide variety of additional services to its customers because MPLS VPNs are aware of the Layer 3 addresses at the customer locations. Additionally, MPLS VPNS can still provide the privacy inherent in Layer 2 WAN services.

MPLS VPNs use MPLS unicast IP forwarding inside the SP's network, with additional MPLS-aware features at the edge between the provider and the customer. Additionally, MPLS VPNs use MP-BGP to overcome some of the challenges when connecting an IP network to a large number of customer IP internetworks **Problems** that include the issue of dealing with duplicate IP address spaces with many customers.

The Solution: MPLS VPNs

In particular, the MPLS VPN RFCs define the concept of using multiple routing tables, called Virtual Routing and Forwarding (VRF) tables, which separate customer routes to avoid the duplicate address range issue. This section defines some key terminology and introduces the basics of MPLS VPN mechanics.

MPLS uses three terms to describe the role of a router when building MPLS VPNs. Note that the names used for the routers in most of the figures in this chapter have followed the convention of identifying the type of router as CE, PE, or P, as listed here.

Customer edge (CE)—A router that has no knowledge of MPLS protocols and does not send any labeled packets but is directly connected to an LSR (PE) in the MPLS VPN.

Provider edge (PE)—An LSR that shares a link with at least one CE router, thereby providing function particular to the edge of the MPLS VPN, including IBGP and VRF tables

Provider (P)—An LSR that does not have a direct link to a CE router, which allows the router to just forward labeled packets, and allows the LSR to ignore customer VPNs' routes

The key to understanding the general idea of how MPLS VPNs work is to focus on the control plane distinctions between PE routers and P routers. Both P and PE routers run LDP and an IGP to support unicast IP routing—just as was described in the first half of this chapter. However, the IGP advertises routes only for subnets inside the MPLS network, with no customer routes included. As a result, the P and PE routers can together label switch packets from the ingress PE to the egress PE.

PEs have several other duties as well, all geared toward the issue of learning customer routes and keeping track of which routes belong to which customers. PEs exchange routes with the connected CE routers from various customers, using either EBGP, RIP-2, OSPF, or EIGRP, noting which routes are learned from which customers. To keep track of the possibly overlapping prefixes, PE routers do not put the routes in the normal IP routing table— instead, PEs store those routes in separate per-customer routing tables, called VRFs. Then the PEs use IBGP to exchange these customer routes with other PEs—never advertising the routes to the P routers. Figure shows the control plane concepts.

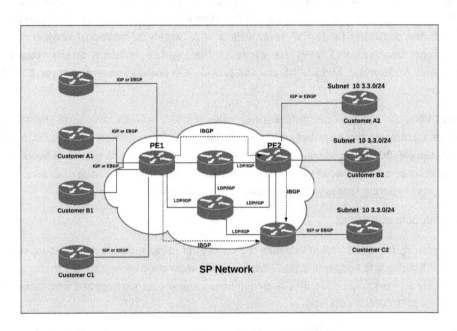

Figure 21 Overview of the MPLS VPN Control Plane

NOTE

The term global routing table is used to refer to the IP routing table normally used for forwarding packets, as compared with the VRF routing tables.

57. What is difference between l2vpn and l3vpn?

Actually, the IP network works over MPLS. The idea of MPLS is that a series of labels can be applied to a given packet (or frame) that can subsequently be used to switch it through a network. In the case of an L3VPN that means that rather than the traditional mechanism of looking at the destination IP address, routing devices look at one or more previously applied labels to make forwarding decisions.

The key point in the above is that the actual -contents- of the packet aren't actually considered. Once a given packet is labeled the intervening devices simply forward it based on whatever LSP has been signaled. In the case of an L3VPN, the packet is a fully formed IP packet. In the case of an L2VPN a frame from a particular interface has a label added and is forwarded. This might be a full Ethernet frame (with or without an 802.1q header), an HDLC frame from a serial link, one or more cells from an ATM PVC, etc.

One of the contrasts between L2 and L3 VPN is the mechanism used to signal and set up the overlay network. L3VPN (RFC2547bis) extends the BGP protocol to allow PE's to signal which routes are available within which VPN's. There are more possible ways to put together a layer 2 network (i.e. straight point-to-point links, multipoint, translational, etc.) and there are also more mechanisms in use in the industry used to signal these various topologies

58. What is Layer 3 VPN (L3VPN)?

Layer 3 VPN (L3VPN) is a type of VPN mode that is built and delivered on OSI layer 3 networking technologies. The entire communication from the core VPN infrastructure is forwarded using layer 3 virtual routing and forwarding techniques.

Layer 3 VPN is also known as virtual private routed network (VPRN).

Layer 3 VPN typically utilizes border gateway protocol (BGP) to send and receive VPN-related data. L3VPN works by enabling VPN clients to peer with the core router. L3VPN utilizes virtual routing and forwarding (VRF) techniques to create and manage user data.

It is built using a combination of IP- and MPLS-based networking technologies. It is generally used to send data on back-end VPN infrastructures, such as for VPN connections between data centers or back offices.

59. What is L2VPN over Metro Ethernet?

The deployment is very lucid and trouble-free. As per the diagram customer is terminated on ME switch with Q-in-Q functionality. The focal advantage of using Q-in-Q in Metro Ethernet circuits to make customer frames unique within L2 domain and preserves the customer vlans. The flow is given below: -

CPE will forward the frames to PE switch with vlan tagging, after receiving the frames PE switch will encapsulate a more vlan tag on the existing vlan tag (It is like label within label of layer 3 VPN). There after a sub interface is created on router physical interface by taking the same VLAN as sub interface and xconnect is created over Ethernet domain by taking remote PE loopback as destination. When the frame is received by remote PE it will tag the frame again by preserving the existing customer vlan and forward to the Metro Domain. Wherever the packet will get out form the access port the upper tag of service provider domain will be removed and customer will able to get the VLAN tag which was being originated.

Why this type connectivity is being asked by service provider? Really awesome question, every service provider doesn't want to lose the confidentiality of its esteemed customers and used to promise their customers that they are Omni. Whenever customer demands the circuit at some remote locations and SP is not feasible on that location at that time layer 2 VPN services comes mostly in picture. One SP asks another SP to provide the layer 2 circuit which looks like to customer that the whole backbone is being used by their service provider.

Monitoring of L2 circuits are not possible.

60. What is E-VPN (Ethernet VPN)?

The Ethernet virtual private network (EVPN) introduces a new model for Ethernet services delivery. It has been dubbed the next-generation all-in-one VPN. With it, you can achieve network simplicity, agility, and scale. All these features are essential in the era of cloud-scale networking. An EVPN does the job of many legacy VPN technologies and does it better than each them in a one-to-one comparison.

61. Advantages of MPLS.

The benefits of an MPLS network are not restricted to the scalability of the network. It also provides: Improved up-time – By providing alternative network paths. Improved bandwidth utilization – By allowing for multiple traffic types to traverse the network.

11. QOS

1. What is QoS and why it is required?

Quality of service (QoS) refers to a network's ability to achieve maximum bandwidth and deal with other network performance elements like latency, error rate and uptime. The primary goal of quality of service is to provide priority to networks, including dedicated bandwidth, controlled jitter, low latency and improved loss characteristics.

2. What are layer2 QoS and layer3 QoS?

Layer 2 QoS uses CoS (class of service) and deals with mac address like

- mac address filter
- mac address mapping
- avoid mac address flooding

Layer 3 QoS uses ToS (type of service) and deals with ip address like

- IP precedence
- usually known as DSCP
- uses AF values
- mainly used for Voice Packets

3. What is tail drop?

Tail drop is a simple queue management algorithm used by network schedulers in network equipment to decide when to drop packets. With tail drop, when the queue is filled to its maximum capacity, the newly arriving packets are dropped until the queue has enough room to accept incoming traffic.

4. Describe methods of QoS?

Differentiated services as defined in RFC 2474

- Traffic policing
- In-profile and out-of-profile packet marking
- Traffic shaping
- Metering
- Integrated services for client and server applications as defined in RFC 1633
- RSVP signaling (RFC 2205)
- Guaranteed service (RFC 2212)
- Controlled-Load service (RFC 2211)
- Policy-based networking
- RAPI shared library for application

5. **Difference between a policer and a shaper?**

The difference between shaping and policing is what happens to traffic that exceeds the configured rate of traffic. With policing, this traffic is either marked down (to be dropped later) or explicitly dropped. With shaping, this traffic is held back or delayed, through queueing, until there is free bandwidth to send it.

Shaping is usually used to ensure a smooth constant rate or transfer. It is also used in cases where you have a slow WAN link from a SP. The SP is enforcing a policer that will drop traffic exceeding your contracted rate. To prevent excess traffic from being dropped, you can configure a shaper on the link towards the SP. The Shaper will queue excess traffic preventing it from being dropped by the SP.

6. **What is token bucket algorithm?**

This is used to try to control the behavior of streams on the IP-networks. By granting a stream a fixed number of tokens per time interval, one can effectively limit its bursts and the number of packets it can send. One has to spend one token per packet sent out on the network; the tokens are thus used to pay for ones use of network resources.

7. **What is the difference between priority and bandwidth command?**

Bandwidth command defines the minimum bandwidth reservation for a specific class when the network is congested. Priority command defines what is the maximum bandwidth reserved for a specific class when the network is congested.

8. **What is low latency queueing?**

Low-latency queuing (LLQ) is a feature developed by Cisco to bring strict priority queuing (PQ) to class-based weighted fair queuing (CBWFQ). LLQ allows delay-sensitive data (such as voice) to be given preferential treatment over other traffic by letting the data to be de-queued and sent first.

9. **What is class based weighted fair queuing?**

Class-based weighted fair queueing (CBWFQ) extends the standard WFQ functionality to provide support for user-defined traffic classes. For CBWFQ, you define traffic classes based on match criteria including protocols, access control lists (ACLs), and input interfaces. Packets satisfying the match criteria for a class constitute the traffic for that class. A queue is reserved for each class, and traffic belonging to a class is directed to the queue for that class.

10. **What is first in first out queue (FIFO)?**

FIFO is an acronym for first in, first out, a method for organizing and manipulating a data buffer, where the oldest (first) entry, or 'head' of the queue, is processed first.

11. What is fair queue?

Fair queuing is a family of scheduling algorithms used in some process and network schedulers. The algorithm is designed to achieve fairness when a limited resource is shared, for example to prevent flows with large packets or processes that generate small jobs from consuming more throughput or CPU time than other flows or processes.

12. If I give the IP precedence five to data traffic, what will happen?

When designing QoS for a network, the precedence 5 is used for real-time traffic. Routers within the network are configured to provide low-latency, low-jitter, and low-loss service to such packets.

13. What's the aim of queuing?

Queuing is meant to accommodate temporary congestion on a network device's interface by storing excess packets in buffers till information measure becomes accessible. Cisco IOS routers support many queueing ways to fulfill the varied information measure, jitter, and delay necessities of various applications.

12. SECURITY

1.   **What is a firewall?**

A firewall is a network security device that monitors incoming and outgoing network traffic and decides whether to allow or block specific traffic based on a defined set of security rules. A firewall can be hardware, software, or both.

2.   **Describe, generally, how to manage a firewall.**

Firewalls that protect enterprise networks play a crucial role on the front line of defense. The people who administer these firewalls have a lot of responsibility in seeing that only the right kind of traffic gets through when it should and all the bad stuff gets blocked. The stakes are high and there's little room for error. But year after year, the Verizon Data Breach Investigations Report shows that device misconfigurations are a leading source of vulnerabilities that open the door to data breaches.

The most common firewall challenges that lead to misconfigurations or other problems that cause firewalls to fail in their crucial missions. The following recommendations:

- Keep the enterprise security policy manager or compliance manager in the loop on firewall changes.
- Clean up unused rules.
- Eliminate conflicting rules.
- Follow a consistent workflow for requesting and implementing firewall changes.

Let's take a look at each recommendation.

Keep the enterprise security policy manager or compliance manager in the loop on firewall changes.

Clean up unused rules.

It's not uncommon for a firewall to have hundreds or even thousands of rules, many of which are outdated and no longer serve the purpose for a business requirement. Unused rules sometimes harbor the potential for malicious attacks. For example, suppose a port is opened to allow HTTP or even HTTPS traffic to flow between the enterprise and a cloud application. Then the business unit that used that cloud application abandons it but fails to notify the firewall administrator to close the port. A malicious attacker could discover that opening and use it to transmit data out of the organization.

There are firewall management tools that can easily monitor the network traffic on an ongoing basis and determine if there are open connections that haven't been used for a specified period of time. The firewall administrator can be alerted to these apparently unused connections to research their purpose and close the ones that no longer serve a business purpose.

Eliminate conflicting rules.

Many firewalls already have such a complex rule base that oftentimes an administrator doesn't know if he or she is implementing a new rule that conflicts with an existing one. This situation could cause the new rule to be completely dysfunctional because the device – acting on the principle of "first match" – executes the first rule it encounters that meets the criteria of the traffic. Cleaning up conflicting rules is not something to tackle manually, however there are tools that can facilitate this task.

Follow a consistent workflow for requesting and implementing firewall changes.

Firewall rules often are not properly documented. Without good documentation, it can be hard to tell who requested a rule or who owns it from a business perspective. This makes it more difficult to comply with regulations such as PCI DSS because it is more difficult to prove that the rule is needed. If there is traffic over that connection, it can be a challenge to know who owns it and for what purpose.

The remediation requires more than a simple tool. It requires the enterprise to define a business process whereby every time a firewall rule is needed there is a workflow that has to be followed. This workflow would include a business owner submitting the access request, someone reviewing and approving the request, and eventually a firewall administrator actually pushing out the change—all while the underlying system documents the change and correlates it to the business need. For future cleanup optimization, there is that business context and the firewall administrator knows who to call to see if the request made a few years ago is still needed today

3.   What is a Denial of Service attack?

A denial-of-service (DoS) is any type of attack where the attackers attempt to prevent legitimate users from accessing the service. In a DoS attack, the attacker usually sends excessive messages asking the network or server to authenticate requests that have invalid return addresses. The network or server will not be able to find the return address of the attacker when sending the authentication approval, causing the server to wait before closing the connection. When the server closes the connection, the attacker sends more authentication messages with invalid return addresses. Hence, the process of authentication and server wait will begin again, keeping the network or server busy.

4.   What is a "spoofed" packet?

IP spoofing is the creation of Internet Protocol (IP) packets which have a modified source address in order to either hide the identity of the sender, to impersonate another computer system, or both. It is a technique often used by bad actors to invoke DDoS attacks against a target device or the surrounding infrastructure. All IP packets contain a header which precedes the body of the packet and contains important routing information, including the source address. In a normal packet, the source IP address is the address of the sender of the packet. If the packet has been spoofed, the source address will be forged.

5. **What is a SYN Flood?**

A SYN flood (half-open attack) is a type of denial of service attack which aims to make a server unavailable to legitimate traffic by consuming all available server resources. By repeatedly sending initial connection request (SYN) packets, the attacker is able to overwhelm all available ports on a targeted server machine, causing the targeted device to respond to legitimate traffic sluggishly or not at all.

6. **What do you do if you are a victim of DoS?**

The function of a denial of service attack is to flood its target machine with too much traffic and prevents it from being accessible to any other requests or providing services.

- To prevent DoS attacks firewall can be configured as a relay; in this approach the firewall responds on behalf of the internal host. During the attack, the firewall responds to the SYN sent by the attacker; since the ACK never arrives, the firewall terminates the connection.
- By Keeping protocols and Antivirus software up-to-date, we can prevent to be a victim of DoS. A regular scanning of the machine is also necessary in order to detect any "anomalous" behavior.

7. **What is GPG/PGP?**

PGP (Pretty Good Privacy) is a public-key encryption program that has become the most popular standard for email encryption. In addition to encrypting and decrypting email, PGP is used to sign messages so that the receiver can verify both the identity of the sender and the integrity of the content. PGP uses a private-key that must be kept secret and a public-key that sender and receiver must share. GPG (Gnu Privacy Guard) is an independent implementation of the OpenPGP standards.

8. **What is SSH?**

SSH, also known as Secure Shell or Secure Socket Shell, is a network protocol that gives users, particularly system administrators, a secure way to access a computer over an unsecured network. SSH also refers to the suite of utilities that implement the SSH protocol.

9. **What is SSL? How do you create certificates?**

SSL Certificates are small data files that digitally bind a cryptographic key to an organization's details. When installed on a web server, it activates the padlock and the https protocol and allows secure connections from a web server to a browser. Typically, SSL is used to secure credit card transactions, data transfer and logins, and more recently is becoming the norm when securing browsing of social media sites.

An organization needs to install the SSL Certificate onto its web server to initiate a secure session with browsers. Once a secure connection is established, all web traffic between the web server and the web browser will be secure.

When a certificate is successfully installed on your server, the application protocol (also known as HTTP) will change to HTTPs, where the 'S' stands for 'secure'. Depending on the type of certificate you purchase and what browser you are surfing the internet on, a browser will show a padlock or green bar in the browser when you visit a website that has an SSL Certificate installed. A website with an SSL Certificate installed look like.

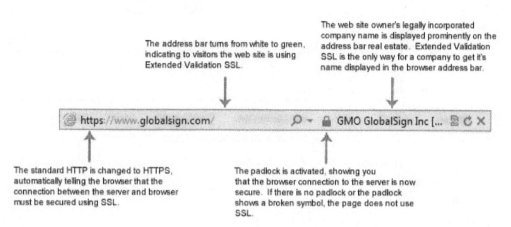

Overview

The following is an extremely simplified view of how SSL is implemented and what part the certificate plays in the entire process.

Normal web traffic is sent unencrypted over the Internet. That is, anyone with access to the right tools can snoop all of that traffic. Obviously, this can lead to problems, especially where security and privacy is necessary, such as in credit card data and bank transactions. The Secure Socket Layer is used to encrypt the data stream between the web server and the web client (the browser).

SSL makes use of what is known as asymmetric cryptography, commonly referred to as public key cryptography (PKI). With public key cryptography, two keys are created, one public, one private. Anything encrypted with either key can only be decrypted with its corresponding key. Thus, if a message or data stream were encrypted with the server's private key, it can be decrypted only using its corresponding public key, ensuring that the data only could have come from the server.

If SSL utilizes public key cryptography to encrypt the data stream traveling over the Internet, why is a certificate necessary? The technical answer to that question is that a certificate is not really necessary - the data is secure and cannot easily be decrypted by a third party. However, certificates do serve a crucial role in the communication process. The certificate, signed by a trusted Certificate Authority (CA), ensures that the certificate holder is really who he claims to be. Without a trusted signed certificate, your data may be encrypted, however, the party you are communicating with may not be whom you think. Without certificates, impersonation attacks would be much more common.

Step 1: Generate a Private Key

The openssl toolkit is used to generate an RSA Private Key and CSR (Certificate Signing Request). It can also be used to generate self-signed certificates which can be used for testing purposes or internal usage.

The first step is to create your RSA Private Key. This key is a 1024 bit RSA key which is encrypted using Triple-DES and stored in a PEM format so that it is readable as ASCII text.

openssl genrsa -des3 -out server.key 1024

Generating RSA private key, 1024 bit long modulus
....++++++
........++++++
e is 65537 (0x10001)
Enter PEM pass phrase:
Verifying password - Enter PEM pass phrase:

Step 2: Generate a CSR (Certificate Signing Request)

Once the private key is generated a Certificate Signing Request can be generated. The CSR is then used in one of two ways. Ideally, the CSR will be sent to a Certificate Authority, such as Thawte or Verisign who will verify the identity of the requestor and issue a signed certificate. The second option is to self-sign the CSR, which will be demonstrated in the next section.

During the generation of the CSR, you will be prompted for several pieces of information. These are the X.509 attributes of the certificate. One of the prompts will be for "Common Name (e.g., YOUR name)". It is important that this field be filled in with the fully qualified domain name of the server to be protected by SSL. If the website to be protected will be https://public.akadia.com, then enter public.akadia.com at this prompt. The command to generate the CSR is as follows:

openssl req -new -key server.key -out server.csr

Country Name (2 letter code) [GB]:**CH**
State or Province Name (full name) [Berkshire]:**Bern**
Locality Name (eg, city) [Newbury]:**Oberdiessbach**
Organization Name (eg, company) [My Company Ltd]:**Akadia AG**
Organizational Unit Name (eg, section) []:**Information Technology**
Common Name (eg, your name or your server's hostname) []:**public.akadia.com**
Email Address []:**martin dot zahn at akadia dot ch**
Please enter the following 'extra' attributes

to be sent with your certificate request
A challenge password []:
An optional company name []

Step 3: Remove Passphrase from Key

One unfortunate side-effect of the pass-phrased private key is that Apache will ask for the pass-phrase each time the web server is started. Obviously, this is not necessarily convenient as someone will not always be around to type in the pass-phrase, such as after a reboot or crash. mod_ssl includes the ability to use an external program in place of the built-in pass-phrase dialog, however, this is not necessarily the most secure option either. It is possible to remove the Triple-DES encryption from the key, thereby no longer needing to type in a pass-phrase. If the private key is no longer encrypted, it is critical that this file only be readable by the root user! If your system is ever compromised and a third party obtains your unencrypted private key, the corresponding certificate will need to be revoked. With that being said, use the following command to remove the pass-phrase from the key:

cp server.key server.key.org
openssl rsa -in server.key.org -out server.key

The newly created server.key file has no more passphrase in it.

-rw-r--r-- 1 root root 745 Jun 29 12:19 server.csr
-rw-r--r-- 1 root root 891 Jun 29 13:22 server.key
-rw-r--r-- 1 root root 963 Jun 29 13:22 server.key.org

Step 4: Generating a Self-Signed Certificate

At this point you will need to generate a self-signed certificate because you either don't plan on having your certificate signed by a CA, or you wish to test your new SSL implementation while the CA is signing your certificate. This temporary certificate will generate an error in the client browser to the effect that the signing certificate authority is unknown and not trusted.

To generate a temporary certificate which is good for 365 days, issue the following command:

openssl x509 -req -days 365 -in server.csr -signkey server.key -out server.crt
Signature ok
subject=/C=CH/ST=Bern/L=Oberdiessbach/O=Akadia AG/OU=Information
Technology/CN=public.akadia.com/Email=martin dot zahn at akadia dot ch
Getting Private key

Step 5: Installing the Private Key and Certificate

When Apache with mod_ssl is installed, it creates several directories in the Apache config directory. The location of this directory will differ depending on how Apache was compiled.

cp server.crt /usr/local/apache/conf/ssl.crt
cp server.key /usr/local/apache/conf/ssl.key

Step 6: Configuring SSL Enabled Virtual Hosts

```
SSLEngine on
SSLCertificateFile /usr/local/apache/conf/ssl.crt/server.crt
SSLCertificateKeyFile /usr/local/apache/conf/ssl.key/server.key
SetEnvIf User-Agent ".*MSIE.*" nokeepalive ssl-unclean-shutdown
CustomLog logs/ssl_request_log \
  "%t %h %{SSL_PROTOCOL}x %{SSL_CIPHER}x \"%r\" %b"
```

Step 7: Restart Apache and Test

```
/etc/init.d/httpd stop
/etc/init.d/httpd stop
```

https://public.akadia.com

10.   **What would you do if you discovered a UNIX or Network device on your network has been compromised?**

Here are the most important steps that Internet Security and IT experts advise you take, if you've been hacked or suspect that an organization you do business with has been attacked:

1. Change your passwords. Make them tricky and hard to guess.

Hackers love stealing email addresses and passwords, together or individually, because they know that most people are predictable and will use the same password for different accounts. If they get only the email address, they count on people using simple passwords that are easy to crack (1234, etc.). That's why you need to change the password you used for the company that's been hacked... along with your other passwords. (Does that sound like a hassle? Well, if you don't use the same passwords for different accounts, it won't be.) By changing passwords, you might avoid having your account hacked.

2. Take a close look at the "hacked" account.

If you heard there'd been a prowler in your neighborhood, you'd be sure to double-check that all the doors in your house were locked. It would also be a good idea to check if the prowler hasn't already come in your home and taken a few things without your being aware of it! Similarly, if you hear of a major hack, take a close look at your account activity with that company, and others. If you use the same username and passwords, you could find that hackers have already gotten into other accounts. You may have to do account recovery or repair in several areas.

3. Get your account back to normal status.

Major companies such as Facebook, Twitter, and Microsoft have experience responding to hackers' attacks, which means they have a process for helping you get your account back to normal if it has been compromised.

If there HAS been a problem, they'll notify you by email and tell you what to do. Just BE SURE of two things:

There has been a documented attack.

The persons reaching out to you via email are indeed with the company! Verify that everything is legitimate before proceeding.

4. Tell friends and family you've been hacked.

You're not looking for sympathy here or sharing bad news—you're alerting people you communicate with that your email account has been hacked and that the hacker may send strange messages in your name, looking for more victims. Your message to friends should simply be, "Keep your eyes open and your guard up if you see suspicious emails from me!"

5. Keep an eye on your financial or credit accounts.

It happens all the time. Hackers get just enough information to hack into a credit or debit card account to make fraudulent purchases (usually online) where they can get away with it. Hopefully, your bank has systems in place to track suspicious activity. You can do your part by opening up your at-risk accounts and checking your account activity yourself. You'll know better than anyone if a purchase was yours or authorized by you or not.

6. Scan your computer for viruses and malware.

If you believe hackers have somehow gotten into your email account, you need to find out if they've gotten into your computer with malware (dangerous software that can take over your computer). You'll want to run a security scan of your computer using a leading antivirus program and malware detector, which can help you find and eliminate any programs lurking on your hard drive, waiting to do more damage.

7. Reinstall your operating system and backup data.

If you suffered a legitimate hack on your system, you may want to consider reinstalling your operating system, wiping your hard drive clean and retrieving your backup files. Unless you're technically savvy and comfortable with the idea, you may want to get help from an IT professional—someone you trust. Because the last thing you want is to transfer damaged files from an infected PC or hard drive to a new one.

Back to normal. Maybe.

Those are the steps you'll need to take if you suspect or know that your computer or personal information has been compromised. Hopefully, you've been able to avoid that drama so far.

To continue staying safe, it's important to break old habits that put you at risk and develop new practices, many of them simple steps. You can keep hackers out of your life by making it harder for them to find a way in and shoring up your defenses when you hear that they're hard at work.

11.   **What would you do if you discovered a Windows system on your network has been compromised?**

First, protect yourself

This is where I repeat the standard litany of "stay safe" advice:

- Use security software like anti-malware tools.
- Keep your software up to date.
- Know how and when to secure your internet connection.
- Stay educated about the latest threats and safe internet behavior.

Prevention is much more effective by far than any attempt to detect a malicious intrusion, either during or after the event.

Clues

If you suspect you have been or are being hacked, the first thing to do is to run scans with your anti-malware tools. Make sure both the programs and their databases are up to date and run full scans of your entire computer.

The most important thing to do is change your passwords.

Reset your passwords

Your account details are what most hackers want. If you cannot log into your account, try resetting your password. If resetting your password or the e-mail address associated with the account no longer work, look for an account recovery option. If all these options fail, you must contact the company directly to have them intervene.

When changing your password, keep the considerations below in mind:

- Make your passwords more complex; add numbers and symbols to them. Passwords like 1234, password, etc. are easy to guess.
- Don't use passwords that you've used in the past.

If you are using the same password for other accounts (which is not advised), you will need to change your other account passwords to be something different. Once a hacker determines your username and password, that information is can be used to compromise other accounts.

If you have a difficult time remembering all your passwords, use a password manager to store them safely.

If two-factor authentication is available, we highly recommend using it.

Check your machine

Make sure to scan your computer for any spyware and malware that may be stealing your account details or logging your keystrokes. If malware is found on your computer, you may want to reset your account passwords again, as infections may have logged your new password.

Verify account details

After you've changed your passwords, ensure that any shipping information is still your address.

If the account authorizes any third-party programs or apps (e.g., Facebook and Twitter), make sure they don't have rights you have not granted. Our best advice is to delete any app you are unfamiliar with or do not remember installing.

Let your other contacts know about the hack
If your e-mail account or any account with contacts is hacked, let your contacts know. Hackers often gain access to other accounts by using affiliated accounts since people are not as suspicious of e-mails coming from someone they know.

Verify past posts
If your social network (e.g., Google+, Twitter, or Facebook) was hacked, make sure there are no posts or messages that have been made on your behalf. Social network accounts are hacked to help spread spam, malware, and advertisements.

New accounts setup
If a hacker gains access to your e-mail, they often use it to set up new accounts. Check your inbox, sent items, and trash for any notifications that a new account was created using your e-mail address. If new accounts have been created, you can try logging into them by using the reset password feature and then delete the account.

12.   What is DNS Hijacking?

Domain Name Server (DNS) hijacking, also named DNS redirection, is a type of DNS attack in which DNS queries are incorrectly resolved in order to unexpectedly redirect users to malicious sites. To perform the attack, perpetrators either install malware on user computers, take over routers, or intercept or hack DNS communication.

13.   What is a log host?

Loghost alias is used by syslog to determine where to send its messages. Check /etc/syslog.conf for ifdef (`LOGHOST',) entries.

14.   What is IDS or IDP, and can you give me an example of one?

Intrusion Detection System (IDS) is the combination of hardware and software that monitors a network or system. Intrusion Detection System (IDS) is used for detecting any malicious activity.

15.   Why are proxy servers useful?

Proxy servers act as a firewall and web filter, provide shared network connections, and cache data to speed up common requests. Proxy servers can provide a high level of privacy. Proxy servers can interpret network traffic, so they are used to cache web pages and files, making it easier and faster for users to access them.

16.   What is web-caching?

Web caching is the activity of storing data for reuse, such as a copy of a web page served by a web server. It is cached or stored the first time a user visits the page and the next time a user requests the same page, a cache will serve the copy, which helps keep the origin server from getting overloaded.

17.   **Accessing Wi-Fi dishonestly is a cyber-crime.**

a) True
b) False

Answer: a

Explanation: Under section 66 of IT Act, 2000 which later came up with a much broader and precise law (as IT Act, 2008) says that if any individual access anyone's Wi-Fi network without the permission of the owner or for doing a malicious activity, it is a cyber-crime.

13. Load Balancers

1. Explain in your own words what is a load balancer.

Load balancing is the process of distributing network traffic across multiple servers. This ensures no single server bears too much demand. By spreading the work evenly, load balancing improves application responsiveness. It also increases availability of applications and websites for users. Modern applications cannot run without load balancers. Over time, software load balancers have added additional capabilities including security and application.

As an organization meets demand for its applications, the load balancer decides which servers can handle that traffic. This maintains a good user experience

Load balancers manage the flow of information between the server and an endpoint device (PC, laptop, tablet or smartphone). The server could be on-premises, in a data center or the public cloud. The server can also be physical or virtualized. The load balancer helps servers move data efficiently, optimizes the use of application delivery resources and prevents server overloads. Load balancers conduct continuous health checks on servers to ensure they can handle requests. If necessary, the load balancer removes unhealthy servers from the pool until they are restored. Some load balancers even trigger the creation of new virtualized application servers to cope with increased demand.

Traditionally, load balancers consist of a hardware appliance. Yet they are increasingly becoming software-defined. This is why load balancers are an essential part of an organization's digital strategy.

2. What are the Algorithms of Load Balancing?
There is a variety of load balancing methods, which use different algorithms best suited for a particular situation.

1) **Least Connection Method:** directs traffic to the server with the fewest active connections. Most useful when there are a large number of persistent connections in the traffic unevenly distributed between the servers.

2) **Least Response Time Method**: directs traffic to the server with the fewest active connections and the lowest average response time.

3) **Round Robin Method**: rotates servers by directing traffic to the first available server and then moves that server to the bottom of the queue. Most useful when servers are of equal specification and there are not many persistent connections.

4) **IP Hash:** the IP address of the client determines which server receives the request.

Load balancing has become a necessity as applications become more complex, user demand grows and traffic volume increases. Load balancers allow organizations to build flexible networks that can meet new challenges without compromising security, service or performance.

3. What are the Benefits Load Balancing?

Load balancing can do more than just act as a network traffic cop. Software load balancers provide benefits like predictive analytics that determine traffic bottlenecks before they happen. As a result, the software load balancer gives an organization actionable insight. These are key to automation and can help drive business decisions.

In the seven-layer Open System Interconnection (OSI) model, network firewalls are at levels one to three (L1-Physical Wiring, L2-Data Link and L3-Network). Meanwhile, load balancing happens between layers four to seven (L4-Transport, L5-Session, L6-Presentation and L7-Application).

Load balancers have different capabilities, which include:

1) **L4** directs traffic based on data from network and transport layer protocols, such as IP address and TCP port.
2) **L7** adds content switching to load balancing. This allows routing decisions based on attributes like HTTP header, uniform resource identifier, SSL session ID and HTML form data.
3) **GSLB** Global Server Load Balancing extends L4 and L7 capabilities to servers in different geographic locations.
4) More enterprises are seeking to deploy cloud-native applications in data centers and public clouds. This is leading to significant changes in the capability of load balancers. In turn, this creates both challenges and opportunities for infrastructure and operations leaders.

4. What are the Types of Load Balancing?
1) Load balancing using SDN
2) A UDP load balancer
3) A TCP load balancer
4) Server Load Balancing (SLB)
5) Virtual load balancing
6) Elastic Load Balancing
7) Geographic load balancing
8) Multi-site load balancing
9) Load Balancer as a Service (LBaaS)

- **Load balancing using SDN** (software-defined networking) separates the control plane from the data plane for application delivery. This allows the control of multiple load balancing. It also helps the network to function like the virtualized versions of compute and storage. With the centralized control, networking policies and parameters can be programmed directly for more responsive and efficient application services. This is how networks can become more agile.

- **A UDP load balancer** utilizes User Datagram Protocol (UDP). UDP load balancing is often used for live broadcasts and online games when speed is important and there is little need for error correction. UDP has low latency because it does not provide time-consuming health checks.

- **A TCP load balancer** uses transmission control protocol (TCP). TCP load balancing provides a reliable and error-checked stream of packets to IP addresses, which can otherwise easily be lost or corrupted.

- **Server Load Balancing (SLB)** provides network services and content delivery using a series of load balancing algorithms. It prioritizes responses to the specific requests from clients over the network. Server load balancing distributes client traffic to servers to ensure consistent, high-performance application delivery.

- **Virtual load balancing** aims to mimic software-driven infrastructure through virtualization. It runs the software of a physical load balancing appliance on a virtual machine. Virtual load balancers, however, do not avoid the architectural challenges of traditional hardware appliances which include limited scalability and automation, and lack of central management.

- **Elastic Load Balancing** scales traffic to an application as demand changes over time. It uses system health checks to learn the status of application pool members (application servers) and routes traffic appropriately to available servers, manages fail-over to high availability targets, or automatically spins-up additional capacity.

- **Geographic load balancing** redistributes application traffic across data centers in different locations for maximum efficiency and security. While local load balancing happens within a single data center, geographic load balancing uses multiple data centers in many locations.

- **Multi-site load balancing**, also known as global server load balancing (GSLB), distributes traffic across servers located in multiple sites or locations around the world. The servers can be on-premises or hosted in a public or private cloud. Multi-site load balancing is important for quick disaster recovery and business continuity after a disaster in one location renders a server inoperable.

- **Load Balancer as a Service (LBaaS)** uses advances in load balancing technology to meet the agility and application traffic demands of organizations implementing private cloud infrastructure. Using an as-a-service model, LBaaS creates a simple model for application teams to spin upload balancers. [14]

5. Does load balancing increase bandwidth?

In computer networking, load balancing aims to optimize connectivity, maximize bandwidth, minimize latency, and avoid the overload of any single Internet connection. By using multiple connections with load balancing, users are able to improve reliability and availability through redundancy. Load balancing usually involves dedicated software or hardware, such as special routers or switches.

The load balancing setup for home users includes special networking hardware (routers), which are embedded with dedicated balancing software. Of course, the router has to be connected to at least 2 WAN Internet connections in order to employ its 'balancing' functionality.

How Load Balancing Works

When you use apps on your devices, information travels to the internet through network sockets – think of them as tubes. A load balancer works by distributing these sockets across all of the Internet connections you are currently using. In this way, load balancing prevents overloading a single connection, thereby increasing overall performance.

So, as long as your apps use lots of sockets, a load balancer does its job and you get faster Internet. General web browsing and torrenting are the most common scenarios for which load balancing should be sufficient.

However, other activities that use only a single network socket to connect to the Internet will not be optimized through load balancing. For instance, video streaming, VPN connections, and large file transfers are not sped up by a load balancer. [15]

6. **Maximum path load balanced by eigrp?**

In general, load balancing is the capability of a router to distribute traffic over all the router network ports that are the same distance from the destination address. Load balancing increases the utilization of network segments, and so increases effective network bandwidth. There are two types of load balancing:

1) Equal cost path – applicable when different paths to a destination network report the same routing metric value. The maximum-paths command determines the maximum number of routes that the routing protocol can use. Maximum-path 6
Router(config-router) #maximum-paths 6

2) Unequal cost path – applicable when different paths to a destination network report are of different routing metric values. The variance command determines which of these routes is used by the router.

7. **How EIGRP support unequal load balancing?**

EIGRP supports up to six unequal-cost paths.
Router(config-router)#variance n

8. **Who does load-balancing when there are multiple links to a destination?**

Load balancing is a standard functionality of the cisco IOS router software, and is available across all router platforms. It is inherent to the forwarding process in the router and is automatically activated if the routing table has multiple paths to a destination. It is based on standard routing protocols, such as routing information protocol (rip), ripv2, enhanced interior gateway routing protocol (EIGRP), open shortest path first (OSPF), and interior gateway routing protocol (IGRP), or derived from statically configured routes and packet forwarding mechanisms. It allows a router to use multiple paths to a destination when forwarding packets. [16]

9. How to use load balancing during system design interviews?

1) Load balancing enables elastic scalability and redundancy (you can have many copies of the same data). Elastic scalability improves performance and throughput of data. Redundancy improves availability and also helps in backup/restore of service in case a few servers fail.

2) Load balancers can be placed at any software layer – refer to the section above for details.

3) Load balancers can be implemented in hardware or software. Many companies use both at different scale points in their system.

10. What is the difference between Per-Destination and Per-Packet Load-Balancing?

1) Per Destination:

This is the default load balancing method enabled on the router. Packets for a given source-destination host pair will take the same path, even if multiple paths are available. For example, given two paths to the same network, all packets for destination1 on that network go over the first path; all packets for destination2 on that network go over the second path, and so on If the majority of the traffic is for a single (source, destination) pair, all traffic will use the same path leaving other paths not utilized.

2) Per Packet:

With Per-packet load-balancing enabled, the router sends one packet for destination1 over the first path, the second packet for (the same) destination1 over the second path, and so on Per packet load balancing is used to avoid path congestion and for insuring equal utilization for all paths to the same destination. However, it may result in out-of-order packets in the data stream which may introduce some problems to sensitive applications like voice or video.

short answer:

- Per-Packet: use for defrag the bandwidth
- Per-Destination: use to defrag the priority

Case1: you have many branch work with one system which your company use it to much … so this case is better to use per-destination, so you can let your user to use first line "15MB" for your system, and5 MB to use internet.

Case2: you need to give one department best connection speed and others you can give them normal speed.

So here you can use Per-Packet

11. Deferential between Load balancer vs DNS vs floating IP.

The difference between floating IPs, DNS, and load balancing are discuss below.

1) DNS:

If you add multiple DNS entries for a domain or subdomain then they the DNS server will randomize the responses and send traffic to the listed IP addresses. This doesn't give you failover protection, but it does provide an easy way to build horizontal scaling, and also if you do experience an issue instead of all of your traffic being lost, you will only lose a percentage. Say 33% if one of three servers fail.

2) **Floating IPs:**

Floating IPs are basically a network configuration where an IP can switch between two servers almost instantaneously. This provides failover and especially if you just have two servers running, one in active, one in passive mode. The problem is that you need to run a service on both servers that are constantly monitoring each other so that they can pass the IP back and forth. It adds fail over protection, but it also creates a potential point of failure.

3) **Load balancing:**

Load balancing is really doing two things. One is that it can be used to create failover protection, but it's also necessary if a single server can't handle all of your requests. This way you can load balance between multiple servers.

However, again you have another point of failure, which is why people setup load balancers in pairs so that if one fails the other one takes over.

The setup with most failover protection would be a floating IP that resides between two load balancers in an active / passive configuration which are then sending traffic back to your actual webservers.

So, you went from one web server to a total of 5 servers pretty quickly, and each one adds a point of failure and you are relying on software to mitigate that.

There are also no services which will be fool proof always and remember the more failover protection you add the more complex the management of your configuration becomes.

So, with that in mind you may want to use a Load Balancer from Digital Ocean as that provides you with a pair of load balancers with a floating IP between them and then you can tell it which backend servers to route requests to.

12. **What is DNS Load Balancing and Why do you need it in a Network?**

Load balancing is commonly used to balance traffic across redundant systems, like web or application servers. So, if one server is unavailable, there are multiple other servers ready to take over the traffic load.

Load balancing can do some pretty amazing things, like:

- Outage protection
- Improve load times
- Reduce server load
- Seamless app rollouts or network expansions

Failover only uses the redundant systems if the primary is unavailable. While load balancing cycles through all the IP addresses in the configuration.

Because failover isn't scalable. As your traffic loads increase, you can't continue to rely on a single system. Let's say you get on Shark Tank and all the sudden your primary web server can't handle your website traffic. It will crash and your users will be sent to your backup web server.

But now your backup is crumbling under the weight of the traffic... and you've just lost thousands of dollars in potential clients.

Load balancing handles these situations better by evenly spreading the traffic load across multiple systems. If a system is unavailable, it will stop sending traffic to it.

14. Additional Questions

1. **What are IGPs and EGPs and why are they different?**

   Interior Gateway Protocols such as RIP, OSPF, IGRP, EIGRP and IS-IS are used within the network of a single organization or a part of an organization, Exterior Gateway Protocols such as EGP and BGP are used for routing between different organizations or "administrative domains".

2. **What do BGP, eBGP, iBGP and AS stand for? What's the difference between eBGP and iBGP?**

   Border Gateway Protocol, internal BGP, external BGP, Autonomous System. eBGP is used towards other autonomous systems, iBGP is used within an AS.

3. **Name several path attributes and their function.**
   1) **Next hop:** contains the IP address of the router where packets for the destination prefix should go to
   2) **AS path**: loop detection, best path selection, to apply filters/policy
   3) Local preference: best path selection / to communicate preference to other routers within the AS
   4) **Multi exit discriminator (MED):** first tie breaker for path selection, originally to select one path when several are available from the same neighbor AS but now often to select the best path between several paths with the same AS path length, regardless of whether they were learned from the same neighbor AS
   5) **Origin:** shows where information in BGP came from (IGP, EGP or unknown), no real/official use but can be used for traffic engineering
   6) Community: one or more 32-bit values with user-defined meanings
   7) **Atomic aggregate:** indicates that a router has aggregated several routes into a larger block
   8) **Aggregator:** indicates where an aggregate route was created

4. **Why is there a problem with iBGP in large networks? How can this problem be solved? Describe each solution in 1 - 3 sentences.**
   1. There must be a full mesh of iBGP sessions, in other words: each BGP router within an AS must have iBGP sessions with all other BGP routers in the AS. By requiring that all information in iBGP is learned directly from the router that learned the information over eBGP, there can't be any loops in iBGP. The full mesh requirement can be solved using either route reflectors or confederations.
   2. **Route reflectors** distribute iBGP information from one router to another, which is normally not allowed in iBGP. Since the clients of the route reflector get all iBGP from the route reflector they don't need to have iBGP sessions with all other BGP routers. Reflectors add additional path attributes that allow them to detect and eliminate loops.

3. In a **confederation**, the AS is split into a number of sub-ASes, so the iBGP full mesh is done within each sub-AS and a modified version of eBGP is used between sub-ASes. To the outside, the confederation behaves like a single AS.

5. **What is the difference between iBGP and eBGP and describe the issues with each?**

Parameter	eBGP	iBGP
Abbreviation for	External BGP	Internal BGP
Neighborship	Both the Routers forming eBGP neighborship need to be in separate AS (Autonomous Systems)	Both the Routers forming iBGP neighborship need to be in same AS (Autonomous Systems)
Route advertisement	A route learnt from an eBGP peer will be advertised back to another IBGP or eBGP neighbor by default.	A route learnt from an IBGP peer will not be advertised back to another IBGP neighbor by default.
As Path addition	AS path is prepended to route when advertised to eBGP peer	AS path is not prepended to the route when advertised to an IBGP peer.
Attributes	Attributes like local preference are not sent to the eBGP peers but are sent to iBGP peer.	Attributes like local preference are sent to the IBGP peers but not to an EBGP peer.
Scope	Used Between organization or between organization and Internet Service provider	Used within the same organization
TTL	By default, EBGP peers are set with TTL = 1, which means neighbors are assumed to be directly connected	By default, EBGP peers are set with TTL = 255
AD (Administrative Distance)	EBGP routes have administrative distance of 20	IBGP routes have administrative distance of 200
Next Hop attribute	Next hop is changed to local router when it is advertised to EBGP peer by default	Next hop remains unchanged when route is advertised to IBGP peer
Topology	Doesn't require full mesh neighborship	Requires full mesh or else either of Route reflectors or Confederation
Loop prevention mechanism	Utilizes As Path for loop prevention	Uses BGP Split horizon i.e. non advertisement from IBGP to IBGP neighbor.

6. **Unlike all other routing protocols, BGP uses TCP as its transport protocol. Discuss the consequences of running BGP over UDP. (What would happen and/or what would have to be changed in BGP.)**

In order to be able to run over UDP, BGP would have to implement functionality that is normally associated with transport protocols, such as retransmissions and reordering. Since in BGP communication is always with specific neighbors that are known in advance, using TCP here allows for a simpler implementation.

7. **What are the disadvantages of existing and proposed BGP security mechanisms?**

BGP TCP MD5 option: hard to implement on general purpose systems, hard to manage because password must match on both sides with no provisions for setting up/changing it, only protects session between two routers, information in BGP may still be wrong.

S-BGP and soBGP: currently, there is no repository of known prefix-to-AS mappings that these protocols could secure. Experience with cryptographic authentication shows there are regularly mistakes that lead to information that is valid being rejected because of a problem with the authentication.

S-BGP: the amount of extra memory in routers and the number of signature checks can be problematic for existing routers, and offloading isn't possible. Secret key must be stored on the router to be able to generate signature

8. **What is recursive lookup in BGP and how it works?**
The router looks up the BGP route and the BGP next hop to reach a destination in the remote AS. Then the router looks up the route to reach the BGP next hop using the IGP.

9. **Can I run two BGP process on single router?**
No, you cannot run two BGP process on a Single Router.

10. **What is the purpose of route dampening?**
Route dampening minimizes the impact of route flaps in downstream autonomous systems upon local and upstream autonomous systems.

11. **In general, which routes will affect by route dampening?**
Route dampening affects only EBGP routes.

12. **What is the purpose of BGP?**
The main purpose of BGP is to exchange routing updates like other routing protocols, but BGP typically does not exchange individual network routes (but it technically can), it exchanges summaries of network routes. This is because the typical use of BGP is over very large networks including the Internet.

13. **What is the BGP path selection criteria?**
BGP tries to narrow its path selection down to one best path; it does not load balance by default. To do so, it examines the path attributes of any loop-free, synchronized (if synchronization is enabled) routes with a reachable next-hop in the following order:

Choose the route with the highest weight.
- If weight is not set, choose the route with the highest local preference.
- Choose routes that this router originated.
- Choose the path with the shortest Autonomous System path.
- Choose the path with the lowest origin code (i is lowest, e is next, ? is last).
- Choose the route with the lowest MED, if the same Autonomous System advertises the possible routes.
- Choose an EBGP route over an IBGP route.

- Choose the route through the nearest IGP neighbor as determined by the lowest IGP metric.
- Choose the oldest route
- Choose a path through the neighbor with the lowest router ID.
- Choose a path through the neighbor with the lowest IP address.

14. What is route reflector and why it is required?

A route reflector is BGP router that is allowed to break the iBGP loop avoidance rule. Route reflectors can advertise updates received from an iBGP peer to another iBGP peer under specific conditions.

By breaking the rules, route reflectors are used to eliminate the full mesh requirement and allow for building iBGP networks that scale easily and cleanly.

15. Precision Time Protocol (PTP)

The Precision Time Protocol, as defined in the IEEE-1588 standard, provides a method to precisely synchronize computers over a Local Area Network (LAN). PTP is capable of synchronizing multiple clocks to better than 100 nanoseconds on a network specifically designed for IEEE-1588.

16. Python script - Can you read, modify & troubleshoot

YABGP is a yet another Python implementation for BGP Protocol. It can be used to establish BGP connections with all kinds of routers (include real Cisco/HuaWei/Juniper routers and some router simulators like GNS3) and receive/parse BGP messages for future analysis.

Support sending BGP messages (route refresh/update) to the peer through RESTful API. YABGP can't send any BGP update messages by itself, it's just an agent, so there can be many agents and they can be controlled by a controller.

We write it in strict accordance with the specifications of RFCs.
This software can be used on Linux/Unix, Mac OS and Windows systems.

Features
It can establish BGP session based on IPv4 address (TCP Layer) in active mode (as TCP client);
Support TCP MD5 authentication (IPv4 and does not support Windows now);
BGP capabilities support: 4 Bytes ASN, Route Refresh(Cisco Route Refresh), Add Path send/receive;
- Address family support:
- IPv4/IPv6 unicast
- IPv4/IPv6 Labeled Unicast
- IPv4 Flowspec(limited)
- IPv4 SR Policy(draft-previdi-idr-segment-routing-te-policy-07)
- IPv4/IPv6 MPLSVPN
- EVPN (partially supported)
- Decode all BGP messages to json format and write them into files in local disk(configurable);

- Support basic RESTFUL API for getting running information and sending BGP messages.

Quick Start

We recommend run yabgp through python virtual-env from source code or pip install

Use yabgp from source code:

```
$ virtualenv yabgp-virl
$ source yabgp-virl/bin/activate
$ git clone https://github.com/smartbgp/yabgp
$ cd yabgp
$ pip install -r requirements.txt
$ cd bin
$ python yabgpd -h
```

Use pip install

```
$ virtualenv yabgp-virl
$ source yabgp-virl/bin/activate
$ pip install yabgp
$ which yabgpd
/home/yabgp/yabgp-virl/bin/yabgpd
$ yabgpd -h
```

17. **How to manipulate bgp routes?**

Route filtering is a method for selectively identifying routes that are advertised or received from neighbor routers. Route filtering may be used to manipulate traffic flows, reduce memory utilization, or to improve security. For example, it is common for ISPs to deploy route filters on BGP peering to customers. Ensuring that only the customer routes are allowed over the peering link prevents the customer from accidentally becoming a transit AS on the Internet.

18. **Do internal BGP sessions behave differently than external BGP sessions?** (Yes)

BGP uses the same concept: If a BGP session is established between two neighbors in different autonomous systems, the session is external BGP (EBGP), and if the session is established between two neighbors in the same AS, the session is internal BGP (IBGP).

19. **What BGP attributes can you use to influence traffic entering your network?** (AS Path, MED, Communities, Origin Type)

20. **What is the command to see IPv6 BGP neighbors?**

To display information about IPv6 Border Gateway Protocol (BGP) connections to neighbors, use the **show bgp ipv6 neighbors command** in user EXEC or privileged EXEC mode.

show bgp ipv6 {unicast | multicast} neighbors [ipv6-address] **[received-routes | routes | flap-statistics | advertised-routes | paths** regular-expression **| dampened-routes]**

21. **The eBGP & iBGP routers, how does select the best router when packets coming in & going out?**

22. **What will be the administrative distance of OSPF routes?**
Administrative distance is the feature that routers use in order to select the best path when there are two or more different routes to the same destination from two different routing protocols. Administrative distance defines the reliability of a routing protocol. Each routing protocol is prioritized in order of most to least reliable (believable) with the help of an administrative distance value.

This table lists the administrative distance default values of the protocols that Cisco supports:

Protocol	Administrative Distance
Connected interface	0
Static route	1
Enhanced Interior Gateway Routing Protocol (EIGRP) summary route	5
External Border Gateway Protocol (BGP)	20
Internal EIGRP	90
IGRP	100
OSPF	110
Intermediate System-to-Intermediate System (IS-IS)	115
Routing Information Protocol (RIP)	120
Exterior Gateway Protocol (EGP)	140
On Demand Routing (ODR)	160
External EIGRP	170
Internal BGP	200
Unknown*	255

Table 15 lists the administrative distance default values

23. **In BGP, what is the purpose of AS_PATH attribute?**
BGP AS_PATH is a well-known mandatory attribute. This attribute identifies the autonomous systems (ASes) through which the UPDATE message has passed. It lists in reverse order the ASes traversed by a prefix, with the last AS placed at the beginning of the list.

24. **What is the BGP path selection criteria?**
Border Gateway Protocol (BGP) routers typically receive multiple paths to the same destination. The BGP best path algorithm decides the best path to install in the IP routing table and to use for traffic forwarding.

25. **Explain loop prevention mechanism in BGP?**
When BGP updates travel through different Autonomous Systems (AS), EBGP routers prepend their AS to AS PATH attribute. BGP routers use this information to check through which Autonomous Systems certain updates passed. If a EBGP speaking router detects its own AS in AS PATH attribute update, the router will ignore the update and will not advertise it further to IBGP neighbors, because it is a routing information loop. This is a built in mechanism for loop prevention in BGP.

26. **Do we need to follow 3-way handshake process to establish BGP communication?**
Yes

27. **Explain LSA, LSU & LSR?**
   - **LSA**: Link state advertisement; It is a message that communicates the router's local routing topology to all other local routers in the same OSPF area. This LSA has types depend on the type of router and has also sequence number.
   - **LSU**: A packet that contains fully detailed LSAs, typically sent in response to an LSR message
   - **LSR**: After exchanging Database Description packets with a neighboring router, a router may find that parts of its topological database are out of date. The Link State Request packet is used to request the pieces of the neighbor's database that are more up to date.

28. **What types of LSAs are filtered between areas?**
Types 1 and 2

29. **What is a type 5 LSA used for?**
External networks not in the OSPF topology

30. **Explain different OSPF LSA types?**
   1) TYPE 1 – ROUTER LSAS: generated by every router in an area and does not cross an ABR
   2) TYPE 2 – NETWORK LSAS: advertised by DR and does not cross an ABR
   3) TYPE 3 – SUMMARY LSAS: Advertised by The ABR Of the Originating Area
   4) TYPE 4 – SUMMARY LSAS: Used to Advertise A Metric to The ASBR And Advertised by The ABR Of the Originating Area
   5) TYPE 5 – AS EXTERNAL LSAS: Used to Advertise Network from Other Autonomous Systems and Is Advertised and Owned by The Originating ASBR (Need Type 4 To Find The ASBR)
   6) TYPE 6 – Multicast OSPF routers flood this Group Membership Link Entry.
   7) TYPE 7 – LSAS DEFINED FOR NOT-SO-STUBBY AREAS (NSSA): Used to Advertise Networks from Other Autonomous Systems Injected into An NSSA Area and Is Advertised and Owned by The Originating ASBR. Translated to Type 5 By the NSSA ABR
   8) TYPE 8 – EXTERNAL ATTRIBUTE LSAS: For BGP
   9) TYPES 9, 10 & 11 – OPAQUE LSAS

31. **What are different neighbor states in OSPF?**
Neighbor adjacencies will progress through several states, including:

   - Down
   - Init State – Routers Multicast Initial Hello (224.0.0.5)
   - Two Way – Routers Send Unicast Hellos Listing Neighbors
   - Exstart – Master/Slave Relationship Established With DR/BDR
   - Exchange – Ddps Are Exchanged
   - Loading – Lsrs For Specific Networks
   - Full – All Lsdbs Are Synchronized With DR/BDR. Routers Are Able to Route Traffic

32. WHAT ARE THE FOUR OSPF ROUTER TYPES?

- internal routers, whose OSPF interfaces all belong to the same area
- backbone routers, which are internal routers in area 0 area
- border routers, which have OSPF interfaces in more than one area autonomous system boundary routers, which advertise external routes into the OSPF domain.

33. WHAT ARE THE FOUR OSPF PATH TYPES?
- Intra-Area Paths
- Inter-Area Paths
- Type 1 External Paths
- Type 2 External Paths

34. WHAT ARE THE FIVE OSPF NETWORK TYPES?
- Point-To-Point Networks
- Broadcast Networks
- Non-Broadcast Multi-Access (NBMA) Networks
- Point-To-Multipoint Networks
- Virtual Links

35. WHAT IS A DESIGNATED ROUTER?
a designated router is a router that represents a multiaccess network, and the routers connected to the network, to the rest of the OSFP domain.

36. HOW DOES A CISCO ROUTER CALCULATE THE OUTGOING COST OF AN INTERFACE?
cisco IOS calculates the outgoing cost of an interface as 108/bw, where bw is the configured bandwidth of the interface.

37. Explain the different modes of OSPF operation

1) BROADCAST – CISCO EXTENSION
2) NONBROADCAST (NBMA) – RFC 2328
3) POINT-TO-MULTIPOINT – RFC 2328
4) POINT-TO-MULTIPOINT NONBROADCAST – CISCO EXTENSION
5) POINT-TO-POINT – CISCO EXTENSION

BROADCAST – CISCO EXTENSION:
- Has One IP Subnet
- Uses Multicast OSPF Hello Packets to Discover Neighbors
- Elects DR And BDR
- Requires A Full-Mesh or Partial-Mesh Topology

NONBROADCAST (NBMA) – RFC 2328:
- Has One IP Subnet
- Requires Neighbors to Be Manually Configured

- Elects DR And BDR
- Requires That the DR and Br Have Full Connectivity with All Other Routers
- Typically Used in A Full-Mesh Or Partial-Mesh Topology

POINT-TO-MULTIPOINT – RFC 2328:
- Has One IP Subnet
- Uses Multicast OSPF Hello Packets to Discover Neighbors
- Does Not Require DR And BDR
- Typically Used in A Partial-Mesh or Star Topology

POINT-TO-MULTIPOINT NONBROADCAST – CISCO EXTENSION:
- Used in Place of RFC Compliant Point-To-Multipoint If Multicast and Broadcast Are Not Enabled On The Virtual Circuit
- Requires Neighbors to Be Manually Configured
- Does Not Require DR And BDR

POINT-TO-POINT – CISCO EXTENSION:
- Unique Subnet on Each Sub interface
- Does Not Have DR And BDR
- Used When Only Two Routers Need to Form an Adjacency On A Pair Of Interfaces
- Can Be Used with Either LAN or Wan Interfaces

38. **WHAT IS THE DIFFERENCE BETWEEN A STUB AREA, A TOTALLY STUBBY AREA, AND A NOT-SO-STUBBY AREA?**
    - A Stub Area Is an Area into Which No Type 5 LSAs Are Flooded.
    - A Totally Stubby Area Is an Area into Which No Type 3, 4, Or 5 LSAs Are Flooded, With the Exception of Type 3 LSAS To Advertise A Default Route.
    - Not-So-Stubby Areas Are Areas Through Which External Destinations Are Advertised into The OSPF Domain, But into Which No Type 5 LSAS Are Sent by the ABR

39. **Explain what a 3-way handshake is in TCP?**
    A three-way handshake is a method used in a TCP/IP network to create a connection between a local host/client and server. It is a three-step method that requires both the client and server to exchange SYN and ACK (acknowledgment) packets before actual data communication begins.

40. **Explain the difference between OSPF and IEGRP?**
    EIGRP is a protocol designed by cisco mainly for cisco devices while OSPF is an open protocol. EIGRP differs from most other distance vector protocols in that it does not rely on periodic route dumps so it is capable of maintaining its topology table.

41. **How routes are selected in OSPF according to preference?**
    If there are multiple routes to a network with the same route type, the OSPF metric calculated as cost based on the bandwidth is used for selecting the best route. The route with the lowest value for cost is chosen as the best route.

42. **What are the router types in OSPF?**
Within an OSPF area, routers are divided into the following categories.
1) **Internal Router**—A router with that has OSPF neighbor relationships only with devices in the same area.
2) **Area Border Router (ABR)** — A router that has OSPF neighbor relationships with devices in multiple OSPF areas. ABRs gather topology information from their connected areas and distribute it to the backbone area.
3) **Backbone Router**—A backbone router is a router that runs OSPF and has at least one interface connected to the OSPF backbone area. Since ABRs are always connected to the backbone, they are always classified as backbone routers.
4) **Autonomous System Boundary Router (ASBR)**—An ASBR is a router that attaches to more than one routing protocol and exchanges routing information between them.

43. **Why OSPF is called Link State?**
The OSPF protocol is a link-state routing protocol, which means that the routers exchange topology information with their nearest neighbors. The topology information is flooded throughout the AS, so that every router within the AS has a complete picture of the topology of the AS.

44. **What is the benefit of LSA concept in OSPF?**
OSPF and LSA types work together to ensure that network traffic is always routed to its intended destination. Large routing tables and network segments efficiently store routing tables including ones that change often. The technology keeps bandwidth usage low when several routers are on a network.

45. **What is the summary of OSPF?**

All of These Terms Are Important for Understanding the Operation of The OSPF And They Are Used Throughout the Article.

OSPF Is Interior Gateway Protocol (IGP) And Distributes Routing Information Only Between Routers Belonging to The Same Autonomous System (AS).

- **NEIGHBOR:** Connected (Adjacent) Router That Is Running OSPF With the Adjacent Interface Assigned to The Same Area. Neighbors Are Found by Hello Packets.
- **ADJACENCY:** Logical Connection Between Router and Its Corresponding DR And BDR. No Routing Information Is Exchanged Unless Adjacencies Are Formed.
- **LINK:** Link Refers to A Network or Router Interface Assigned to Any Given Network.
- **INTERFACE:** Physical Interface on The Router. Interface Is Considered as Link, When It Is Added To OSPF. Used to Build Link Database.
- **LSA:** Link State Advertisement, Data Packet Contains Link-State and Routing Information, That Is Shared Among OSPF Neighbors.
- **DR:** Designated Router, Chosen Router to Minimize the Number of Adjacencies Formed. Option Is Used in Broadcast Networks.
- **BDR:** Backup Designated Router, Hot Standby for The DR. BDR Receives All Routing Updates from Adjacent Routers, But It Does Not Flood LSA Updates.
- **AREA:** Areas Are Used to Establish A Hierarchical Network.

- **ABR**: Area Border Router, Router Connected to Multiple Areas.
- **ASBR**: Autonomous System Boundary Router, Router Connected to An External Network (In A Different AS).
- **NBMA**: Non-Broadcast Multi-Access, Networks Allow Multi-Access but Have No Broadcast Capability (For Example X.25, Frame Relay). Additional OSPF Neighbor Configuration Is Required for Those Networks.
- **BROADCAST**: Network That Allows Broadcasting, For Example Ethernet.
- **POINT-TO-POINT**: Network Type Eliminates the Need for Drs and BDRS
- ROUTER-ID: IP Address Used to Identify OSPF Router. If the OSPF Router-ID Is Not Configured Manually, Router Uses One of The IP Addresses Assigned to The Router as Its Router-ID.
- **LINK STATE:** The Term Link State Refers to The Status of a Link Between Two Routers. It Defines the Relationship Between A Router's Interface and Its Neighboring Routers.
- **COST** Link-State Protocols Assign A Value to Each Link Called Cost. The Cost Value Is Depend to Speed of Media. A Cost Is Associated with The Outside of Each Router Interface. This Is Referred to As Interface Output Cost.
- **AUTONOMOUS SYSTEM:** An Autonomous System Is A Group of Routers That Use A Common Routing Protocol to Exchange Routing Information.

46. **If you go to Amazon.com how the IP does address get resolved?**
"What happens when you type in a URL" is a deceptive question commonly asked in tech interviews. If you look online, there are many very detailed resources but few concise explanations of how a web browser, a server, and the general internet work together.

This is how I would explain it:

You enter a URL into a web browser

1) The browser looks up the IP address for the domain name via DNS
2) The browser sends a HTTP request to the server
3) The server sends back a HTTP response
4) The browser begins rendering the HTML
5) The browser sends requests for additional objects embedded in HTML (images, css, JavaScript) and repeats steps 3-5.
6) Once the page is loaded, the browser sends further async requests as needed.

That's really it. Here's a description in words for this site.

When you type "https://Amazon.com" into your browser the first thing that happens is a Domain Name Server (DNS) matches "Amazon.com" to an IP address. Then the browser sends an HTTP request to the server and the server sends back an HTTP response. The browser begins rendering the HTML on the page while also requesting any additional resources such as CSS, JavaScript, images, etc. Each subsequent request completes a request/response cycle and is rendered in turn by the browser. Then once the page is loaded some sites (though not mine) will make further asynchronous requests.

If I were asked to explain further, I might start talking about how the server and browser connect via TCP. And we could discuss encryption via https, too.

If you want to know IP add of Amazon.com, open cmd in windows and do nslookup on the website as shown in the following snapshot .

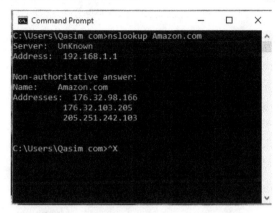

47.   **What are the components of a TCP header?**
TCP headers appear in the following sequence:
- Source TCP port number (2 bytes)
- Destination TCP port number (2 bytes)
- Sequence number (4 bytes)
- Acknowledgment number (4 bytes)
- TCP data offset (4 bits)
- Reserved data (3 bits)
- Control flags (up to 9 bits)
- Window size (2 bytes)
- TCP checksum (2 bytes)
- Urgent pointer (2 bytes)
- TCP optional data (0-40 bytes)

48.   **How to remove the duplicates from the list?**

The job is simple. We need to take a list, with duplicate elements in it and generate another list which only contains the element without the duplicates in them. [17]

Examples:

Input: [2, 4, 10, 20, 5, 2, 20, 4]
Output: [2, 4, 10, 20, 5]

Input: [28, 42, 28, 16, 90, 42, 42, 28]
Output: [28, 42, 16, 90]
Recommended: Please try your approach on {IDE} first, before moving on to the solution.
We can use not in on list to find out the duplicate items. We create a result list and insert only those that are not already in.

```
# Python code to remove duplicate elements
def Remove(duplicate):
final_list = []
for num in duplicate:
if num not in final_list:
final_list.append(num)
return final_list

# Driver Code
duplicate = [2, 4, 10, 20, 5, 2, 20, 4]
print(Remove(duplicate))
```
Output:

[2, 4, 10, 20, 5]

49. What Are the Differences Among Router, Switch and Hub?

Hub (layer 1 Device):

Hubs, also known as repeaters, are network devices that can operate on layer-1 (I.e. the physical layer) to connect network devices for communication.
A common connection point for devices in a network (Physical Layer-Layer1). When a packet arrives at one port, it is copied to the other ports so that all segments of the LAN can see all packets.

Switch (layer 2 Device):

Switches are network devices that operate on layer-2 of OSI model of communication.
Switches are also known as intelligent hubs.
In networks, a device that filters and forwards packets between LAN segments. Switches operate at the data link layer (layer 2) and sometimes the network layer(layer 3) of the OSI Reference Model .

Router (layer 3 Device):

Routers are the network devices that operate at Layer-3 of OSI model of communication.
As layer-3 protocols have access to logical address (IP addresses) so routers have the capability to forward data across networks.
Sometimes routers are also known as layer-3 switches.
A device that forwards data packets along networks. A router is connected to at least two networks, commonly two LANs or WANs or a LAN and its ISP [Network Layer (Layer3)]

50. Name Three Steps Which You Would Use to Troubleshoot Ftp Server Related Problems.?

Test basic connectivity with ping, Check with nmap if the ports are open (20 and 21). Check if a firewall is restricting traffic to the server.

51. How Would You Troubleshoot DNS Problems?

Ping the DNS server and check the response. Check with Wireshark if DNS request and response packets are being sent and received.

52.   Name Three Steps Which You Would Use to Troubleshoot Internet Related Problems.?

Check the connectivity with the default gateway. Check if the DNS server is configured on the PC. Check if the appropriate port number is active using Nmap on the DNS server.

53.   How Would You Troubleshoot DHCP Server Related Issues.?

Check the IP connectivity with the DHCP server from a system configured on the network. Test if the DHCP client and server service is started on the DHCP server and the client. Test if the DHCP server service is reachable using Nmap.

54.   A User Is Unable to Telnet into The Router. Explain the Methodology of Troubleshooting.?

Check the IP connectivity using ping. Check if port 23 is open on the router using Nmap.

55.   A User Is able to Ping Ip Addresses on The Internet, But Unable to Access It Via Domain Names. Should the DNS Server Be Configured on The Gateway or The Client.

The DNS server can be a public server or the gateway address. If it is the gateway address, the DNS server address should be configured on the gateway. The DNS server should also be configured on the users TCP/IP adapter.

56.   What Could Be the Maximum Length of The Lan Cable?

The theoretical length is 100 meters but after 80 meters you may see drop in speed due to loss of signal.

57.   What Would You Use to Connect Two Computers Without Using Switches?

Cross cable.

58.   What Is the Difference Between Physical Address and Logical Address?

Physical Address: It's called as MAC Address (48 bit)

Logical Address: It's Called as Ip Address   (IPv4 -32 bit & IPv6 -128 bit)

59.   Describe what Traceroute does?
Traceroute is a command which can show you the path a packet of information takes from your computer to one you specify. It will list all the routers it passes through until it reaches its destination or fails to and is discarded. In addition to this, it will tell you how long each 'hop' from router to router takes.

In Windows, select Start > Programs > Accessories > Command Prompt. This will give you a window like the one below.

Enter the word tracert, followed by a space, then the domain name.

The following is a successful traceroute from a home computer in New Zealand to mediacollege.com:

```
Command Prompt                                                              _|□|×|

C:\>tracert mediacollege.com

Tracing route to mediacollege.com [66.246.3.197]
over a maximum of 30 hops:

  1    <10 ms    <10 ms    <10 ms  192.168.1.1
  2    240 ms    421 ms     70 ms  219-88-164-1.jetstream.xtra.co.nz [219.88.164.1]
  3     20 ms     30 ms     30 ms  210.55.205.123
  4      *         *          *    Request timed out.
  5     30 ms     30 ms     40 ms  202.50.245.197
  6     30 ms     40 ms     40 ms  g2-0-3.tkbr3.global-gateway.net.nz [202.37.245.140]
  7     30 ms     30 ms     40 ms  so-1-2-1-0.akbr3.global-gateway.net.nz [202.50.116.161]
  8    160 ms    161 ms    160 ms  p1-3.sjbr1.global-gateway.net.nz [202.50.116.178]
  9    160 ms    171 ms    160 ms  so-1-3-0-0.pabr3.global-gateway.net.nz [202.37.245.230]
 10    160 ms    161 ms    170 ms  pao1-br1-g2-1-101.gnaps.net [198.32.176.165]
 11    180 ms    181 ms    180 ms  lax1-br1-p2-1.gnaps.net [199.232.44.5]
 12    170 ms    170 ms    171 ms  lax1-br1-ge-0-1-0.gnaps.net [199.232.44.50]
 13    240 ms    241 ms    240 ms  nyc-n20-ge2-2-0.gnaps.net [199.232.44.21]
 14    240 ms    251 ms    250 ms  ash-n20-ge1-0-0.gnaps.net [199.232.131.36]
 15    241 ms    240 ms    250 ms  0503.ge-0-0-0.gbr1.ash.nac.net [207.99.39.157]
 16    251 ms    260 ms    250 ms  0.so-2-2-0.gbr2.nwr.nac.net [209.123.11.29]
 17    250 ms    260 ms    261 ms  0.so-0-3-0.gbr1.oct.nac.net [209.123.11.233]
 18    250 ms    260 ms    261 ms  209.123.182.243
 19    250 ms    260 ms    261 ms  sol.yourhost.co.nz [66.246.3.197]

Trace complete.

C:\>

◄                                                                        ►
```

Traceroute

Firstly, it tells you that it's tracing the route to mediacollege.com, tells you the IP address of that domain, and what the maximum number of hops will be before it times out.

Next it gives information about each router it passes through on the way to its destination.

- 1 is the internet gateway on the network this traceroute was done from (an ADSL modem in this case)
- 2 is the ISP the origin computer is connected to (xtra.co.nz)
- 3 is also in the xtra network
- 4 timed out
- 5 - 9 are all routers on the global-gateway.net.nz network (the domain that is the internet gateway out of New Zealand)
- 10 - 14 are all gnaps.net in the USA (a telecom supplier in the USA)
- 15 - 17 are on the nac network (Net Access Corporation, an ISP in the New York area)
- 18 is a router on the network mediacollege.com is hosted on
- and finally, line 19 is the computer mediacollege.com is hosted on (sol.yourhost.co.nz)

Each of the 3 columns are a response from that router, and how long it took (each hop is tested 3 times). For example, in line 2, the first try took 240ms (240 milliseconds), the second took 421 ms, and the third took 70ms.

You will notice that line 4 'timed out', that is, there was no response from the router, so another one was tried (202.50.245.197) which was successful.

You will also notice that the time it took quadrupled while passing through the global-gateway network.

This is extremely useful when trying to find out why a website is unreachable, as you will be able to see where the connection fails. If you have a website hosted somewhere, it would be a good idea to do a traceroute to it when it is working, so that when it fails, you can do another traceroute to it (which will probably time out if the website is unreachable) and compare them. Be aware though, that it will probably take a different route each time, but the networks it passes through will generally be very similar.

If the example above had continued to time out after line 9, you could suspect that global-gateway.co.nz was the problem, and not mediacollege.com.

If it timed out after line 1, you would know there was a problem connecting to your ISP (in this case you would not be able to access anything on the internet).

It is generally recommended that if you have a website that is unreachable, you should use both the traceroute and ping commands before you contact your ISP to complain. More often than not, there will be nothing to your ISP or hosting company can do about it.

60.   Describe 192.168.1.24/24 - he was ultimately looking for if the IP was in the middle of a range or a broadcast address?

This is a Class C IP address that cannot be used on the Internet. It is a part of the 24-bit block of private addresses which require either a proxy or address translation to route Internet traffic. This address contains the following information as mention below.

Address	192.168.1.24
Netmask	255.255.255.0 = 24
Wildcard	0.0.0.255
Network	192.168.1.0/24
Broadcast	192.168.1.255
First IP	192.168.1.1
Last IP	192.168.1.254
Hosts/Net	254

61.   What is selective ACK

TCP Selective Acknowledgements (SACK)

Selective Acknowledgements are a refinement of TCP's traditional "cumulative" acknowledgements.

SACKs allow a receiver to acknowledge non-consecutive data, so that the sender can retransmit only what is missing at the receiver's end. This is particularly helpful on paths with a large bandwidth-delay product (BDP).

TCP may experience poor performance when multiple packets are lost from one window of data. With the limited information available from cumulative acknowledgments, a TCP sender can only learn about a single lost packet per round trip time. An aggressive sender could choose to retransmit packets early, but such retransmitted segments may have already been successfully received.

A Selective Acknowledgment (SACK) mechanism, combined with a selective repeat retransmission policy, can help to overcome these limitations. The receiving TCP sends back SACK packets to the sender informing the sender of data that has been received. The sender can then retransmit only the missing data segments.

Multiple packet losses from a window of data can have a catastrophic effect on TCP throughput. TCP uses a cumulative acknowledgment scheme in which received segments that are not at the left edge of the receive window are not acknowledged. This forces the sender to either wait a roundtrip time to find out about each lost packet, or to unnecessarily retransmit segments which have been correctly received. With the cumulative acknowledgment scheme, multiple dropped segments generally cause TCP to lose its ACK-based clock, reducing overall throughput. Selective Acknowledgment (SACK) is a strategy which corrects this behavior in the face of multiple dropped segments. With selective acknowledgments, the data receiver can inform the sender about all segments that have arrived successfully, so the sender need retransmit only the segments that have actually been lost.

The selective acknowledgment extension uses two TCP options. The first is an enabling option, "SACK-permitted", which may be sent in a SYN segment to indicate that the SACK option can be used once the connection is established. The other is the SACK option itself, which may be sent over an established connection once permission has been given by SACK-permitted.

62.   **What is IP Fragmentation and define the Impact on network forwarding?**

IP fragmentation is an Internet Protocol (IP) process that breaks packets into smaller pieces (fragments), so that the resulting pieces can pass through a link with a smaller maximum transmission unit (MTU) than the original packet size. The fragments are reassembled by the receiving host.

RFC 791 describes the procedure for IP fragmentation, and transmission and reassembly of IP packets.[1] RFC 815 describes a simplified reassembly algorithm. The Identification field along with the foreign and local internet address and the protocol ID, and Fragment offset field along with Don't Fragment and More Fragment flags in the IP protocol header are used for fragmentation and reassembly of IP packets.
If a receiving host receives a fragmented IP packet, it has to reassemble the packet and pass it to the higher protocol layer. Reassembly is intended to happen in the receiving host but in practice it may be done by an intermediate router, for example, network address translation (NAT) may need to reassemble fragments in order to translate data streams.

Impact on network forwarding
When a network has multiple parallel paths, technologies like LAG and CEF split traffic across the paths according to a hash algorithm. One goal of the algorithm is to ensure all packets of the same flow are sent out the same path to minimize unnecessary packet reordering.

IP fragmentation can cause excessive retransmissions when fragments encounter packet loss and reliable protocols such as TCP must retransmit all of the fragments in order to recover from the loss of a single fragment. Thus, senders typically use two approaches to decide the size of IP packets to send over the network. The first is for the sending host to send an IP packet of size equal to the MTU of the first hop of the source destination pair. The second is to run the path

MTU discovery algorithm,[6] to determine the path MTU between two IP hosts, so that IP fragmentation can be avoided.

63.   What is layer 2 switching and explain?

- LAYER 2 SWITCHING Is Hardware Based, Which Means It Uses the Media Access Control (MAC) address from the host's network interface cards (NICS) to filter the network. switches use application-specific integrated circuits.

- LAYER 2 SWITCH Traditional Switching Operates at Layer 2 Of the OSI Model, Where Packets Are Sent to A Specific Switch Port Based on Destination MAC Addresses and Devices in The Same Layer 2 Segment Do Not Need Routing to Reach Local Peers.

- On LAYER 2 SWITCHING Protocols and Concepts Used to Improve Redundancy, Propagate VLAN Information, And Secure the Portion of The Network Where Most Users Access Network Services. Switches Only Know the Mac Addresses of The Hosts That Are Either Connected Directly to Their Ports and Have Already Sent At Least 1 Frame or The Mac Addresses of Other Switches That They Are Able to Talk To.

- Layer 2 Forwarding Table -The Destination MAC Is Checked Against the CAM Table to Determine If the Frame Contains A Layer 3 Packet (If the MAC Address Belongs to A Layer 3 interface on the switch).

- LAYER 2 SWITCHING Is So Efficient Because There Is No Modification to The Data Packet, Only to The Frame Encapsulation of The Packet, And Only When the Data Packet Is Passing Through Dissimilar Media (Such as From Ethernet to FDDI).

- Remember That Layer 2 Switches Break Up Collision Domains, But the Network Is Still One Large Broadcast Domain. Layer 2 Switches Break Up Collision Domains on Each Port, But All Ports Are Still Considered, By Default, To Be in One Large Broadcast Domain.

64.   What are the limitations of layer 2 switching?

Layer 2 Switches Have the Same Limitations as Bridge Networks. Remember That Bridges Are Good If You Design the Network by the 80/20 Rule. The Old 80/20 Rule Is That 80% Of the Traffic Was on Their Local Segment and Only 20% Of the Network Traffic Went Over the Backbone (End-To-End VLANs ---> Follow The 80/20 Rule = 80% Local 20 % Across Core).

Bridged Networks Break Up Collision Domains, But the Network Is Still One Large Broadcast Domain. Similarly, Layer 2 Switches (Bridges) Cannot Break Up Broadcast Domains, Which Can Cause Performance Issues and Limits the Size of Your Network. Broadcast and Multicasts, Along with The Slow Convergence of Spanning Tree, Can Cause Major Problems as The Network Grows. Because Of These Problems, Layer 2 Switches Cannot Completely Replace Routers in The Internetwork.

65.   Define NETWORK-DESIGN 80/20 Vs 20/80 Rule:

80/20 Vs 20/80 Rule Is Related to The Traffic Pattern. Does One User/Resource in That Particular VLAN Communicates Mostly Inside the VLAN Or Outside. In the Early Days of Networking Traffic Was Mostly 80/20, Which Dictates That 80 Percent of The Traffic Remains on The Local Network, And Only 20 Percent Should Be Routed to Another Network.

But for Quite A Few Years Now It Has Shifted To 20/80. Because Routing Introduces More Latency Than Switching, the 20/80 Rule Has Dictated A Need for A Faster Layer 3 Technology, Namely Layer 3 Switching

66. **What is layer 3 switching explain?**
    - A Layer 3 Switch, Makes Forwarding Decisions Based on Layer 3 IP Addresses. Layer 3 Switches Are Enhanced Layer 2 Switches And, Hence, Have the Same High Port Densities That Layer 2 Switches Have. Routers on The Other Hand Typically Have A Much Lower Port Density. Layer 3 Switches Allow You to Mix and Match Layer 2 And Layer 3 Switching, Meaning You Can Configure A Layer 3 Switch to Operate as A Normal Layer 2 Switch, Or Enable Layer 3 Switching as Required.
    - A LAYER 3 SWITCH Is A High-Performance Device (Switching Is A Hybrid) For Network Routing. Layer 3 Switches Actually Differ Very Little from Routers. The Only Difference Between A Layer 3 Switch and A Router Is the Way the Administrator Creates the Physical Implementation. Also, Traditional Routers Use Microprocessors to Make Forwarding Decisions, And the Switch Performs Only Hardware-Based Packet Switching.
    - However, Some Traditional Routers Can Have Other Hardware Functions as Well in Some of The Higher-End Models. Layer 3 Switches Can Be Placed Anywhere in The Network Because They Handle High-Performance LAN Traffic and Can Cost-Effectively Replace Routers. A Layer 3 Switch Can Support the Same Routing Protocols as Network Routers Do.

    - There Are Different Types of Layer 3 Switching, Route Caching and Topology-Based. In Route Caching the Switch Required Both A Route Processor (RP) And A Switch Engine (SE). The RP Must Listen to The First Packet to Determine the Destination. At That Point the Switch Engine Makes A Shortcut Entry in The Caching Table for The Rest of The Packets to Follow. Due to Advancement in Processing Power and Drastic Reductions in The Cost of Memory, Today's Higher End Layer 3 Switches Implement A Topology-Based Switching Which Builds A Look Up Table and Populates It with The Entire Network's Topology. The Database Is Held in Hardware and Is Referenced There to Maintain High Throughput. It Utilizes the Longest Address Match as The Layer 3 Destination.

67. **What is Layer 4 Switching and explain?**
    - A Layer 4 Switch Would Take into Consideration L4 Information Regarding Forwarding/Filtering of Data. We Could Say That A Router with ACLs Or Policy Based Routing That Look at Layer 4 Information Regarding Segments of Data Is A Layer 4 Device.
    - LAYER 4 SWITCHING Provides Additional Routing Above Layer 3 By Using the Port Numbers Found in The Transport Layer Header to Make Routing Decisions. These Port Numbers Are Found in Request for Comments (RFC) 1700 And Reference the Upper-

Layer Protocol, Program, Or Application. Layer 4 Information Has Been Used to Help Make Routing Decisions for Quite A While.

- LAYER 4 SWITCHES Are Capable of Identifying Which Application Protocols (HTTP, SNTP, FTP, And So Forth) Are Included with Each Packet, And Use This Information to Hand Off the Packet to The Appropriate Higher-Layer Software.
- Because Layer 4 Devices Enable You to Establish Priorities for Network Traffic Based on Application, You Can Assign A High Priority to Packets Belonging to Your Vital In-House Applications, With Different Forwarding Rules for Low-Priority Packets.
- LAYER 4 SWITCHES Also Provide an Effective Wire-Speed Security Shield for A Network Because Any Company- Or Industry-Specific Protocols Can Be Confined to Only Authorized Switched Ports or Users. This Security Feature Is Often Reinforced with Traffic Filtering and Forwarding Features.
- A LAYER 4 SWITCH Also Must Allocate A Large Amount of Memory to Its Forwarding Tables. Layer 2 And Layer 3 Devices Have Forwarding Tables Based on MAC and Network Addresses, Making Those Tables Only as Large as The Number of Network Devices. Layer 4 Devices, However, Must Keep Track of Application Protocols and Conversations Occurring in The Network. Their Forwarding Tables Become Proportional to The Number of Network Devices Multiplied by The Number of Applications.

68. **What is difference between router and layer3 switch.**

Look at the technical pieces. You have a switch. It switches. It works at Layer 2 and does its fancy data- link/frame stuff and does it very fast! This is good.

You have a router. Its routes. It works at Layer 3 and does its fancy network/packet stuff, and depending on the model you have, does it very fast! This too is good!

Then you have marketing people. They don't know much technically, but they know how to sell things. You have design people too! They know far more about ASICs and ICs then I will ever proclaim to know, but they don't know much about marketing. Putting these two groups together is very scary!

What started out as a great combination of two SEPARATE things (a switch and a router) has suddenly become something akin to Frankenstein. It's something new, built from the pieces of other common things we know and love! But that doesn't make it something different!

The base of an "L3 switch" is still a switch. It will do the same functions as other switches. There is a separate bus architecture for the L3 "stuff" that it does, and in most instances an actual daughterboard that the router is contained on. So, what we have done is placed a router inside the switch. There is still a switching engine that works just like any other switch. There is still a routing engine that works like any other router. They happen to exist in the same box now, which saves rack space, makes things appear sexier than they did before, and gives people new and exciting ways to spend their money!

Now a note! If you're going to an interview, please don't repeat what I just said word for word! Play nice with others and just explain the technical parts: It's simply a combination of two previously separate items!

Don't forget that our routers have always assembled frames and remembered next-hop MAC addresses. Does that make them Layer 2 routers? I think not. Enjoy the power they bring, but don't forget the basics are still the same. Just more horsepower!

69. What is ipconfig?

Ipconfig is a utility program that is commonly used to identify the addresses information of a computer on a network.
It can show the physical address as well as the IP address.

70. In EIGRP, what is a Stuck in Active route?

The EIGRP Stuck in Active event happens when a router that sends a Query message asking for a route does not receive a Reply from an adjacent in a certain amount of time. This time is called the Active time and is set to 180 seconds by default; at half of the active timer, the router that lost the route start sending SIA-Query in order to validate the availability of the adjacent neighbour, if after 90 seconds the router does not receive a SIA-Reply, then the adjacency is dropped.

71. What is difference between Flow Control and Congestion Control?

Both Flow Control and Congestion Control are the traffic controlling methods in different situations.
The main difference between flow control and congestion control is that, in flow control, Network traffics is controlled which flows from sender to a receiver. On the other hand, in congestion control, traffic is controlled entering into the network.

Let's see the difference between flow control and congestion control:

S.NO	FLOW CONTROL	CONGESTION CONTROL
1	In flow control, traffics are controlled which are flow from sender to a receiver.	traffics are controlled entering to the network.
2	Data link layer and Transport layer handle, it.	Network layer and Transport layer handle, it.
3	In this, Traffic is prevented by slowly sending by the sender.	In this, Traffic is prevented by slowly transmitting by the transport layer.
4	In this, Receiver's data is prevented from being overwhelmed.	In this, Network is prevented from congestion.
5	In flow control, Only sender is responsible for the traffic.	In this, Transport layer is responsible for the traffic.

Table 16 Difference between flow control and congestion control

72. Describe the difference between routing and switching?

146

Routing:
Routing moves a letter or telephone call to the access layer (as in a street or telephone exchange).
Switching:
Switching makes the final delivery.
A switching decision is made on the part of the address that is not used in routing (as in the street number or last four digits of a phone number).

73.   **Compare Perl with C**

S#	C	Perl
1	Development tools are less and are not very advanced	There are several development tools in Perl as compare to C
2	C has speed almost equal to that of Perl	It executes in a slower manner than C in a few situations
3	The same is not possible in case of C	Code can be hidden in Perl
4	Additional tools are the prime requirement	Executable can be created without depending on the additional tools

Table 17 Compare Perl with C

74.   **Is it possible in the Perl to use code again and again? If so, which feature enable user to that?**

Yes, it is possible in Perl. However, there is a limit on usage of the same code in the same program. The users need not to worry about the complexity either as Perl is equipped with a code trimming feature. It automatically guides users on how to keep the code as short as possible. Code reusability is a prime example of this. The feature that enables users to simply keep up the pace towards this is "Inheritance". The child class in this feature can use the methods of their parent class.

75.   **How can you represent the warning signs in the Perl in case of an error and what are the options through which this task can be performed?**
There is an option in Perl which is known as WCommand Line. All the warning messages can be displayed using this and the pragma function simply makes sure that the user can declare the variables during appearance of warning messages. The entire program can be scrolled easily and in fact, in a very short span of time using the in-built debugger.

76.   **While writing a program, why the code should be as short as possible?**
Complex codes are not always easy to handle. They are not even easy to be reused. Moreover, finding a bug in them is not at all a difficult job. Any software or application if have complex or lengthy code couldn't work smoothly with the hardware and often have compatibility issues. Generally, they take more time to operate and thus becomes useless or of no preference for most of the users. The short code always makes sure that the project can be made user-friendly and it enables programmers to save a lot of time.

77.   **Can you tell the meaning of the term debugging in the programming?**

Well, every programmer is familiar with this approach. The fact is there are many errors that declare their presence in the programs due to reasons which are not always necessary to be known exactly. Eliminating these errors is very essential for the smooth flow of the tasks. Finding the bugs or the errors is known as debugging. The programming languages can have in-built options for debugging or the programmers are free to consider other options too.

78. **What are "Require" and "Use" statement in Perl and when it is used?**

It is considered when it comes to importing the functions in a way that they can be accessed directly during the program. The users are free to get the results in case the sub statements are not accurate. On the other side, the use statement is generally executed during parsing.

79. **In Perl, is it possible for the programmers to prefer a dynamic approach when it comes to loading the binary extension?**

Yes, it is possible. The only need for this is the system a programmer is using must support it. The other option is to accomplish this task statically in case the system doesn't allow the same. Dynamic approach can help users to save time as they are free to perform some basic tasks in their own way.

80. **Name a few arguments which are used in Perl frequently. Tell their meaning as well**

These are as following
- d which means debug
- w that indicates warning
- e means execute
- c which says non return compilation

81. **While start working on a project, how you will decide Perl is suitable for the same**

The first thing to pay attention to is whether the execution need is fast or not. If so, Perl is a good option to consider. The users are free to keep up the pace with the flexibility as well. Perl is highly flexible and it can enable users to keep up the pace with the same. Perl is open source and is free from licenses issues. Perl has one of the best and in fact largest free code repositories that simply make it one of the best options to be considered. Also, it is one of the best programming languages with a vast support available for the programmers.

82. **Name the operators which are used in Perl and are common?**

1. Assignment Operators
2. Arithmetic Operators
3. Increment operators
4. Comparison operators
5. Logical Operators
6. String Operators

83. **Tell how can an array be made empty in Perl?**
This can be done easily. For this, the value of the array is set to zero and the users can then perform this task by assigning the null list to it.

84. **Tell one reason why Perl aliases are good enough to be considered and is faster than references?**
They don't need dereferencing and that is one of the best things about it. A lot of tasks that are not required or are not usual can be avoided easily.

85. **Tell something about memory management in Perl?**
When the programmers make use of a variable in Perl, some memory get occupies. The users have to make sure that the memory is utilized in the best possible manner. After a program is executed, the files can be divided into the sections easily and can then be managed.

86. **What is Closure in Perl and how it is helpful?**
It is defined as the block of code in Perl which is used for capturing the lexical variable which can be accessed at a later section in a program.

87. **What do you understand by Perl scripting?**
It can be regarded as one an important script programming language similar to that of C and C++ language implemented in the IT market. It is mainly used for network operations. The use of Perl scripting depends on the compiler and not on the interpreter. The Perl is used mainly for network operations, developing websites and OS programs.

88. **What Are the Different Types of Perl Operators?**
There are four different types of Perl operators they are:
  1) Unary operator like the not operator
  2) Binary operator like the addition operator
  3) Tertiary operator like the conditional operator
  4) List operator like the print operator

89. **What are data types that Perl can handle?**
  - Data types that Perl can handle are:
  - Scalars ($): It stores a single value.
  - Arrays (@): It stores a list of scalar values.
  - Hashes (%): It stores associative arrays which use a key value as an index instead of numerical indexes

90. **How would you ensure the re-use and maximum readability of your Perl code?**
Below is the list of points to ensure the re-use and maximum readability of your Perl code:

  - Perl offers USE command to modularize code and it includes wherever it is required in a program

- Perl also offers subroutines or functions. This command is used to segregate operations and helps code to be reused
- Perl use objects to create programs and this object will be reused again and again
- Perl include comments in their syntaxes as per requirement
- Perl eliminates dereferencing operator

91. Why is Perl scripting used?

Perl Scripting is used for designing 76 operating systems at the same time and 3000 modules. Other functional concepts can also be done with the help of this programming language. For extending its support to operating systems and modules, it is also known as comprehensive Perl archive network modules. In simple words, the use of the language is to extract information from any text file and result in a printing form of the same by converting the text file.

92. Explain some advantages and disadvantages of programming using Perl script language?

Advantages – Perl is a high-level programming language that is simpler to understand due to its syntax. It is also easier to use due to its flexibility, and easy readability. In addition, the language also supports OOP. It also becomes easier to understand since it has the ability to combine many languages.

Disadvantages – This software is not portable and has some unreadable codes. It is slower compared to another programming language since it is an interpretative language. When you apply any code which is more than 200 lines, it starts to give in problem within the program. It also contains CPAN module which makes it incompatible to run on the system in which CPAN is not installed.

93. What is the importance of Perl warnings and how to turn them on?

In order to check the quality of any coding in the language, warnings are the basic methods to check the wrong codes. During the lexical analysis stage, some usual mandatory problems are highlighted. Therefore, the time spent for researching weird results are very high which can be minimized by turning on the warnings.

There are several ways to turn on the warnings.
-w option is used on the command line for Perl one-liner
-w option is also used on shebang line on OS such a UNIX or windows. The Windows Perl interpreter does not require warnings.
For another operating system, the compiler warnings should be selected.

94. What is the differentiate between tuples and lists in python?
Answer:
The major difference is tuples are immutable while a list is mutable. It means once you create tuple you cannot edit or make changes in the value in tuple while in a list we can edit the value in it.

Tuples	List
A tuple is a sequence of immutable objects	List are versatile datatype which are Mutable
The syntax for Tuples is shown by parenthesis {}	Syntax for List is shown by square brackets []
They are of fixed length	List can be of variable length
Eg: tup_1 = {10,'john',5}	Eg : list_1 = [10, 'john', 5]

Table 18 Differentiate between tuples and lists

95. Explain the difference Python Shell vs Bash Shell Programming Scripting

Now we have seen how we can combine python and shell scripts to create a chain of commands and execute them together. Now, let's take a step further and see whether Python can totally replace Bash Shell.

Speaking of bash shell programming, in terms of performance, bash totally beats the crap out of python. But if you compare it to data types and other advanced stuff, bash doesn't have much compatibility. The start-up time of a bash shell script is 2.8 milli seconds while that of python is 11.1 milli seconds. Bash is a general-purpose language just like Python, but both have their own strengths and weaknesses. Bash shell programming is the default terminal in most Linux distributions and thus it will always be faster in terms of performance. But does that mean it can totally replace Python? Nope. When dealing with large programs, Bash will keep on getting complicated whereas Python does not. Python can also be used as an Object-oriented language as far as I know. If you are just a beginner, then you might not even know the difference between the two. Python is the most elegant scripting language, even more than Ruby and Perl. Bash shell programming on the other hand is actually very excellent in piping out the output of one command into another.

Shell Scripting is simple, and it's not as powerful as python. It does not deal with frameworks and it's tough to get going with web related programs using Shell Scripting. The real power of shell scripting lies in the Stream Text editor or sed, the AWK Programs and similar apps.

96. What is the difference between Perl and Python?

Perl is a general purpose, high level interpreted and dynamic programming language. It was developed by Larry Wall, in 1987. Perl was originally developed for the text processing like extracting the required information from a specified text file and for converting the text file into a different form. Perl supports both the procedural and Object-Oriented programming. Perl is a lot similar to C syntactically and is easy for the users who have knowledge of C, C++.

Python is a widely used general-purpose, high level programming language. It was initially designed by Guido van Rossum in 1991 and developed by Python Software Foundation. It was mainly developed for emphasis on code readability, and its syntax allows programmers to express concepts in fewer lines of code.

FEATURE	PERL	PYTHON
Introduction	Perl is a general-purpose high-level language popular for CGI scripts. Some of the popular projects in Perl are cPanel and Bugzilla. It was initially designed to replace complex shell scripts.	Python is a widely used general-purpose, high level programming language. Due to its rich library and support, it has wide applications in Web Development, Machine Learning, Desktop Applications, etc.
Whitespaces	Perl does not care about whitespaces.	Python deals with whitespaces and a syntax error generates if whitespaces are not according to Python.
Focus	Perl accentuates support for common tasks such as report generation and file scanning.	Python accentuates support for common methodologies such as object-oriented programming and data structure design.
File Extension	The .pl file extension is used to save Perl Scripts. For example, myDocument.pl	The .py file extension is used to save Python Scripts. Example: myFile.py
Statement Blocks	Perl uses braces to mark the statement blocks.	Python use indentations to mark the statement blocks.
End of Statement	All statements should end with a semi colon in Perl.	It is not necessary to end the statements with a semi colon in Python as it deals with whitespaces.
Datatypes	Some data types contained by Perl are numeric, string, Scalars, Arrays, Hashes.	Some data types contained by Python are numeric, strings, lists, dictionaries, tuples.

Table 19 Difference between Perl and Python

15. NETWORK AUTOMATION

1. What is Network Automation?

Network automation is the process of automating the configuration, management, testing, deployment, and operations of physical and virtual devices within a network. Everyday network tasks and functions are performed automatically. Using a combination of hardware and software-based solutions, large organizations, service providers, and enterprises can implement network automation to control and manage repetitive processes and improve network service availability.

Today, networks are fully capable of undertaking the following tasks:

- Discovering topologies
- Managing bandwidth and finding fast reroutes to implement the best computing paths
- Performing root cause analysis
- Updating and installing routes
- Setting performance benchmarks
- Updating software
- Implementing security and compliance

Working together, automation and orchestration simplify network operations involving complex configurations and devices' management while providing business agility to adapt to an ever-changing environment. You can think of automation as accomplishing repeatable tasks without human intervention, and orchestration as the process of stringing together a series of these tasks to accomplish a process or workflow.

Driving network automation is the rapid expansion of network infrastructure required to support the exponential growth of network traffic generated by video, social media, data, and applications' usage. Additionally, as computing power continues to decline in cost and virtual computing continues to grow, network automation becomes more available to many businesses. Various types of network automation can apply to local area networks, virtualized environments, data centers, and public and private clouds.

2. What are the Automation Benefits?

By automating networking features and implementing software products that offer automation, organizations benefit from the following:

1) Lower costs—Because automation reduces the complexities of your underlying infrastructure, dramatically fewer person-hours are required for configuring, provisioning, and managing services and the network. By simplifying operations, consolidating network services, reducing floor space, and cycling underutilized devices off, you need fewer staff to troubleshoot and repair, and reap power savings.

2) Improve business continuity—By removing the chance for human errors, companies can offer and deliver a higher level of services with more consistency across branches and geographies. For example, Juniper Networks' Service Now is a remote, automated troubleshooting client that

enables Juniper to detect quickly and proactively any problems in a customer's network before they become aware of them.

3) Increase strategic workforce—By automating repetitive tasks subject to human error, companies increase productivity, which helps drive business improvements and innovation. As a result, new job opportunities arise for the existing workforce.

4) Greater insight and network control—Automation helps make IT operations more responsive to change through analytics. You gain more visibility into the network and understand precisely what is happening in your network with the ability to control and adapt as needed.

5) Increase business agility—Automation enables companies to develop operational models that improve time-to-market. You can add new services, test new applications, and fix problems. Time to realize improvements is reduced, resulting in greater competitiveness and elasticity, and ultimately, more profits added to the corporate bottom line.

3. What is the Future of Network Automation?

Looking ahead, networks of the future will be able to accomplish the following:

- Conduct smart-auto-bandwidth
- Implement automatic service placement and service motion
- Provide specific upgrades based on configured services
- Initiates network actions based on machine learning

The route forward toward an autonomous network relies on telemetry, automation, machine learning, and programming with declarative intent. This future network is called the Self-Driving Network™, an autonomous network that is predictive and adaptive to its environment. For more information, read Juniper Networks, The Self-Driving Network™.

To be effective, automation must break free of traditional silos to address all network infrastructure elements, teams, and operations support systems. Juniper Networks offers simplified network architectures as essential components for simplified overall IT operations. Designed with a flexible and open standards-based framework, Juniper Networks tools and strategies help data center infrastructures by enabling automation across the full operations lifecycle—from network provisioning to management to orchestration.

4. What Makes Network Automation Possible?

Automation in networking is possible for three reasons.

1) Generic routing switches
2) Software defined networking (SDN)
3) Infrastructure as Code

Making routers generic is what makes SDN possible. The result was the separation of hardware and software. An example from other tech spaces is hardware and operating system separation in personal computers and mobile devices.

It took some time, but the same change is occurring in networking.

Generic Routing Switches

The first fundamental piece of the networking puzzle is the commodification of hardware. This means switches have to be manufactured so you could write any code on top of them. That means no proprietary software needed to run on hardware. Open source.

This occurred with the introduction of routing switches from Aruba Networks, HP, NoviFlow, and Juniper Networks. As a response to this shift, Cisco is also making generic routing switches.

Generic switches come with the ability to separate hardware from software. This provides the foundation for software defined networking.

Software Defined Networking

Once software could control routing switches, there was the emergence of software defined networking. This is the second core principle that has made networking automation possible.

Software defined networking controls the three separated network layers:

- Management plane
- Control plane
- Data plane

The separation of these layers is what makes controlling routers and network switches with software possible. A popular open source software that makes this possible is OpenFlow. OpenFlow provides the ability to write new routing protocols.

Infrastructure as Code

The last concept in making networking automation work is infrastructure as code. This is the principle, adopted by DevOps, that makes controlling processes and servers possible.

Infrastructure as code is not just about writing scripts to make servers behave the way you like. Infrastructure as code is using software development standards and testing techniques and applying them to coding servers and infrastructure.

The goal is to replicate and scale networking protocols across the entire network. This eliminates repetitive tasks, one-off scripts, as well as prevents "fat fingers".

5. Why do you need network automation?

You need automation in networking for the following reasons:

1) Prevent fat fingers
2) Eliminate repetitive tasks
3) Reproduce and dispose of things
4) Deliver code

6. Give Specific Examples where Python Scripting is being used for Network Automation

As python scripting is a handy tool for network automation, typical manual tasks that can be

automated are:

- Configuring switches
- Configuring routers

- Configuration changes
- Configuration management
- Troubleshooting

We need automation in networking to create a more efficient networking environment, improved network uptime and prevent mistakes. Network Automation is helping to solve:

- Mistakes due to human error in configuring the devices
- Repetitive tasks such as changing device logging credentials or time-based ACLs
- Allows to reproduce and dispose of logs which may cause devices to crash
- Deliver bug free code on time

7. What is Scripting?

Any programming language that supports a script is known as scripting language. It helps programmers in order to write programs for a distinct environment to automate the execution of a number of tasks which could otherwise be executed manually by a human operator, one-by-one. Thus, scripting is baseline of network automation.

Python which is the subject of this book is a high-level programming language which was first released in 1991 and still competing fairly because of its efficient design philosophy. It is a general-purpose programming language which underscores code readability by means of significant whitespace.

Some popular ad useful scripting languages are JavaScript, PHP, Perl, Ruby, TCL, Lua. Among these, Lua is one of the most powerful, swift, and light-weight scripting languages.

8. What are the Differences between Tuples and Lists?

The difference between a list and a tuple is that lists are mutable while the tuples are immutable. Due to this Tuples are simpler, they never change and don't have any of the useful properties found in lists that make working with lists so powerful. Hence if you really don't need what lists have to offer and you just want to create a container for immutable stuff, use tuples instead, since they are simpler and thus, faster.

9. How Python Can Be Used in Software Testing?

To generate test data; parse test results; generate reports; testing API calls etc.

- Python to extract requirements from a Word document.
- For testing tasks automation, setting up environments for tests, extracting performance data, etc....
- Testers use Python extensively in many companies with Selenium for test automation.
- For writing desktop applications used by testers.
- Test data manipulation.
- To build test environment
- Testing with IronPython on .NET

10. **Explain List, Tuple, Set, and Dictionary and provide at least one instance where each of these collection types can be used.**
    - **List:** Collection of items of different data types which can be changed at run time.
    - **Tuple:** Collection of items of different data types which cannot be changed. It only has read-only access to the collection. This can be used when you want to secure your data collection set and does not need any modification.
    - **Set:** Collection of items of a similar data type.
    - **Dictionary:** Collection of items with key-value pairs.
    - Generally, **List and Dictionary** are extensively used by programmers as both of them provide flexibility in data collection.

11. **How does For loop and While loop differ in Python and when do you choose to use them?**
    - **For loop** is generally used to iterate through the elements of various collection types such as List, Tuple, Set, and Dictionary.
    - **While loop** is the actual looping feature that is used in any other programming language. This is how Python differs in handling loops from the other programming languages.

12. **Name some of the important modules that are available in Python.**
    Networking, Mathematics, Cryptographic services, Internet data handling, and Multi-threading modules are prominent modules. Apart from these, there are several other modules that are available in the Python developer community.

13. **Does the same Python code work on multiple platforms without any changes?**

    Yes. As long as you have the Python environment on your target platform (Linux, Windows, Mac), you can run the same code.

14. **What Is Network Automation with Network Virtualization?**

    Network automation with network virtualization is key to SDN and NFV technologies. It is expected to reduce costs and speed up the delivery of network-based services by abstracting configuration information for network services from the physical infrastructure. Thus, services may be set up with automated software orchestration tools.

    As server virtualization did for computing resources, network virtualization enables hardware resources to be split up and controlled by software. This way, network resources can be configured and divided for different customers and services without requiring physical changes or discrete infrastructures.

    Automation and Virtualization

Network automation with network virtualization enables automation by programmatically configuring and provisioning network connections. This is a process known as orchestration. For example, a virtual private network (VPN) could be established by a software controller that orchestrates the compute resources and network hardware needed to provide the service.

Network services are generally programmed using network interfaces and application programming interfaces (APIs) governed by open standards. Using software-defined networking (SDN) and network functions virtualization (NFV) technology, services can be configured or changed based on sets of business or services rules. This defines how the hardware platforms interoperate with each other and enables them to be controlled with software.

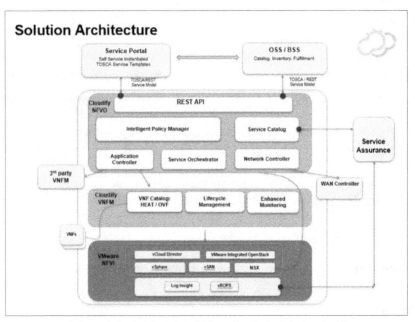

Network Automation with Network Virtualization – Solution Architecture

Orchestration and Management Tools

The trend toward network virtualization has created a new crop of provisioning and management technology, including for cloud network connections, service provider networks, and wide-area networks (WANs).

The primary goal of using network virtualization to automate the network is to remove the need for humans to manually configure pieces of hardware, which in the past has been done by manually typing in configuration information into a command-line interface (CLI) for a hardware device. One way to imagine it is that instead of physically ordering that money be moved by filling out a form in a branch office of a bank, you could just electronically transfer that money to your bank by clicking a button. Network services can also be automatically configured – without the paperwork.

The SDN and NFV movements are building standards so that network configuration and provisioning can be executed with standard software tools and APIs. There are many different standards, APIs, and open source projects emerging to enable the accomplishment of network automation through virtualization.

One standards area includes the European Telecommunications Standards Institute (ETSI) Industry Specification Group (ISG) for NFV Management and Orchestration (MANO) – the ETSI NFV MANO architecture. This is a defined framework for the management and orchestration of all resources in a cloud data center. ETSI NFV MANO includes specific standards for setting up (orchestrating) network services on cloud servers. The data centers host the services using virtualization technology from commercial vendors such as VMware or open source projects such as OpenStack. OpenFlow is an open source protocol for routing packets through a network to access cloud servers.

Other standards and data models are designed to enable automation across SDN and NFV networks. These include Topology and Orchestration Specification for Cloud Applications (TOSCA) – a standard language to describe a topology of cloud-based Web services, components, relationships, and the processes that manage them. YANG (RFC 6020) is a data modeling language developed by the Internet Engineering Task Force (IETF) for configuration and network state information using NETCONF protocol (RFC 6241).

All of these standards and data models can be thought of as a language for SDN or NFV platforms to talk to one another and order provisioning of services without requiring a manual setup – lowering costs and hastening the delivery of new services.

16. FINAL REMARKS – SUGGESTIONS

This book presents a set of questions and answers to potential network engineering candidates to prepare well for their network engineering questions. This is in no way comprehensive or definite guide to cracking an interview but it's a good start.

A Network Engineer should implement topologies and play with several networking technologies either on a real network or a simulated network such as using GNS3, The Boson NetSim Network Simulator or Cisco VIRL.

With this book we have tried to bridge the gap between the interviewer and interviewees by provided an expected answer hence this book is also a reference guide to interviewers to ask the potential candidates the right questions and the key terms that must be included in the network engineering candidates answers.

Today's enterprise and service provider Telecom and IP networks are complex and are designed to fit the various needs. The network designs are not standardized but there has always been a great effort from networking equipment manufacturers, academia and standards bodies to come up with standard designs but it is still far from reality therefore this book includes many network design questions however depending upon the experience and knowledge of the candidates the answers may vary.

Book includes a special section on network Automation which is an advancement in the network engineering field and make network deployments straightforward and scalable.

17. REFERENCES

We have provided list of resources that were used to answer some of the questions in this book. If we are missing a reference to your page, please reach out to us and we will gladly include the references with full credits here.

1. **Introduction**

2. **SCENARIO QUESTIONS**

3. **SWITCHING**

    https://www.brainscape.com/flashcards/ccna-stp-questions-2-1028858/packs/1844894

    https://www.wisdomjobs.com/e-university/spanning-tree-protocol-stp-interview-questions.html

4. **TCP/IP Interview Questions**

    https://www.careerride.com/nw-architecture-of-tcpip-protocol.aspx

5. **IPv6 Interview Questions**

6. **Routing information Protocol (RIP)**

7. **Enhanced Interior Gateway Routing Protocol (EIGRP)**

    https://www.onlinenetworkssolution.com/2017/04/eigrp-interview-questions-and-answer.html.

8. **OSPF**

    https://abhishektechdecoder.wordpress.com/2018/08/20/forwarding-address-fa-in-ospf-lsas

    https://community.cisco.com/t5/switching/multiple-ospf-processes/td-p/1335402.

    https://www.metaswitch.com/knowledge-center/reference/what-is-open-shortest-path-first-ospf.

http://expertsxchange.blogspot.com/2009/02/draw-diagram-of-typical-ospf-network.html

https://learningnetwork.cisco.com/thread/119482

https://learningnetwork.cisco.com/thread/20392

9.   BGP

https://study-ccna.com/designated-backup-designated-router/

https://www.ccexpert.us/bgp-4/route-reflector-clusters.html.

http://www.bgpexpert.com/bgpanswers.php.

10.   MPLS

https://www.cisco.com/c/en/us/td/docs/switches/lan/catalyst6500/ios/12-2SY/configuration/guide/sy_swcg/mpls.pdf

http://www.mplsvpn.info/2010/06/what-is-downstream-and-upstream-router.html.

http://www.mplsvpn.info/2010/06/how-does-label-distribution-protocolldp.html.

http://www.mplsvpn.info/2010/06/is-ldp-required-for-vpnv4-labels.html?m=1.

http://www.ciscopress.com/articles/article.asp?p=1081501&seqNum=4.Section

https://www.cisco.com/c/en/us/td/docs/switches/lan/catalyst9500/software/release/1 6 9/command_reference/b_169_9500_cr/mpls_commands.pdf

http://support.huawei.com/enterprise/docinforeader!loadDocument1.action?contentId=DOC1000142061&partNo=10042

https://ourtechplanet.com/understanding-mpls-basics%E2%80%8B/

http://joannewagnersblog.blogspot.com/2010/09/load-balancing.html?m=1

Layer 3 VPN (L3VPN) https://www.techopedia.com/definition/30757/layer-3-vpn-l3vpn

https://tools.ietf.org/html/rfc3031.

https://mplsvpn.wordpress.com/2010/06/25/is-ldp-required-for-vpnv4-labels/

http://www.mplsvpn.info/2008/12/what-will-happen-if-you-see-your-pe.html

https://techhub.hpe.com/eginfolib/networking/docs/switches/K-KA-KB/16-01/5200-0141_mrg/content/ch17.html

http://www.mplsvpn.info/2010/06/types-of-pseudowire.html

http://www.ciscopress.com/articles/article.asp?p=1081501&seqNum=4

https://serverfault.com/questions/395588/what-is-mpls-layer-2-vpn-and-how-is-it-different-from-mpls-layer-3-vpn https://www.techopedia.com/definition/30757/layer-3-vpn-l3vpn

11. QOS

12. SECURITY

https://support.hpe.com/hpsc/doc/public/display?docId=emr_na-c03651675

13. Load Balancers

https://www.acodersjourney.com/system-design-interview-load-balancing/

https://speedify.com/blog/combining-internet-connections/bonding-vs-load-balancing/.

https://avinetworks.com/what-is-load-balancing/.

https://www.onlinenetworkssolution.com/2017/04/eigrp-interview-questions-and-answer.html.

https://specialties.bayt.com/en/specialties/q/69050/what-is-the-difference-between-per-destination-and-per-packet-load-balancing/

https://www.digitalocean.com/community/questions/load-balancer-vs-dns-vs-floating-ip

http://news.constellix.com/dns-load-balancing-what-is-it-and-why-do-you-need-it/

14. Additional Questions

https://wiki.geant.org/display/public/EK/SelectiveAcknowledgements

https://en.wikipedia.org/wiki/IP_fragmentation

https://mindmajix.com/perl-scripting-interview-questions

https://wsvincent.com/what-happens-when-url/

15. Network Automation

https://www.juniper.net/us/en/products-services/what-is/network-automation/

https://datapath.io/resources/blog/what-is-network-automation/

https://www.softwaretestinghelp.com/python/python-interview-questions/

https://www.sdxcentral.com/networking/virtualization/definitions/what-is-network-automation-with-network-virtualization/

16. Final Remarks – Suggestions

17. References

www.ingramcontent.com/pod-product-compliance
Lightning Source LLC
Chambersburg PA
CBHW071250050326
40690CB00011B/2329